For Pamela Collingwood,

with sincere regards,

Edward Wakeling

November 1996.

LEWIS CARROLL'S DIARIES

THE PRIVATE JOURNALS OF

CHARLES LUTWIDGE DODGSON

(LEWIS CARROLL)

The first complete version of the nine surviving volumes

with notes and annotations

BY

EDWARD WAKELING

VOLUME 2

Containing Journal 4
January to December 1856

The Lewis Carroll Society: Publications Unit

1994

First published in 1994

Published by

THE LEWIS CARROLL SOCIETY

Publications Unit

36 Bradgers Hill Road, Luton, Beds, LU2 7EL.

British Library Cataloguing in Publication Data
The Private Journals of Charles Lutwidge Dodgson
The Lewis Carroll Society: Publications Unit
1. Carroll, Lewis - Biography
2. Authors, English - 19th century
I. Wakeling, Edward
ISBN 0 904117 07 3

Printed at the L. & T. Press, Luton, Beds

Introduction

The journal for October to December 1855, Dodgson's third volume, is missing, presumed lost or destroyed. The one surviving entry for December 31 which was quoted by Collingwood in his *Life and Letters of Lewis Carroll* (T. Fisher Unwin: 1898) is reprinted in the first volume of this series. Nine of the original thirteen journals survive and this series will publish all these entries together with the additional extracts used by Collingwood from the four journals which have since been lost. Entries for January to December 1856 appeared in Dodgson's fourth journal, and this is printed here for the first time in its entirety.

Dodgson's activities during the three months for which the diary is missing are unaccounted for. No letters or papers survive from this period. We only have a brief reference in Collingwood which indicates that he was made a Master of the House on October 15, 1855 in honour of the appointment of the new Dean, Henry George Liddell, who succeeded Dean Thomas Gaisford. Collingwood explains that this conferment entitled Dodgson to all the privileges of a Master of Arts within the walls of Christ Church (p.58). Dodgson did not gain his M.A. from the University until 1857. We do know that Dodgson was appointed Mathematical Lecturer by the new Dean (see *Diary 1,* Dodgson's note dated August 20, 1855 which was appended to his entry for March 24, p.79) to commence during the autumn (Michaelmas) term. This task, alone, must have been time consuming, giving Dodgson little opportunity for other activities as he prepared for his lectureship. The formalities of the role did not begin until January 1856.

During this period, Dodgson was still compiling *Mischmasch*, the eighth and last of the domestic magazines. Of the twenty-five written entries and numerous illustrations in this repository of Dodgson's early literary writings and publications, some are dated during the three months from October to December 1855. "Hints for Etiquette: or Dining Out made Easy" appeared in *The Comic Times* dated October 13, 1855. This parody of good table manners was written in September 1855 (see *Diary 1*, p.131) and appears in *Mischmasch* as a cutting from *The Comic Times*. Dodgson's other contribution to this new and humorous penny rival to *Punch* during this period was "Photography Extraordinary," also written in September (see *Diary 1*, p.132) and published in the issue dated November 3, 1855. This, too, was pasted into *Mischmasch* at a later date. "The Palace of Humbug" was written at Oxford towards the end of 1855. This humorous poem was refused by *The Comic Times*, *The Train* and *Punch*. Its fate is chronicled here (see January 10 & February 5, 1856) eventually being published in *The Oxford Critic* in May 1857.

Dodgson was at Croft at the end of September 1855 when *Diary 1* breaks off. He spent some time earlier that month visiting the Wilcox aunts, uncles and cousins at Whitburn, and during this time it is possible that he wrote "Stanza of Anglo-Saxon Poetry" which eventually became the first stanza of "Jabberwocky" in *Through the Looking-Glass* (1871). There is no specific mention of this poem in *Diary 1*, but it appears in *Mischmasch*, signed and dated "Croft 1855." A few items in *Mischmasch* are undated and some may have been composed during these three months at the end of 1855.

The penultimate page of this journal is missing. There is an outside chance that this is due to mis-numbering, although I incline to the view that the page has been removed, probably by Dodgson himself. He is reflecting on the events of 1856 and with the last day of the year slipping by, he takes the opportunity to confess his shortcomings in the pages of his journal. This is a spontaneous personal action which occurs without reflection; he simply bares his soul and records all his misdeeds. These must be judged in the context of Victorian values and his Christian upbringing. He records sloth, wasting time, lack of regularity in his actions, inattention to his new position as mathematical lecturer, and other shortcomings which many people today would take as very minor faults. Yet, to Dodgson, these were serious enough to warrant heartfelt resolutions for change. My guess is that he had second thoughts about his list of personal transgressions and chose to remove them himself, dwelling more on his proposed future actions. He may have written little on the missing page. The fact that the next existing page begins anew with his thoughts on his future resolutions tends to support this notion. There is, of course, a possibility that the page was removed at a later time, by an unknown censor. We know that other pages in the journal have been cut out, and some of these are at crucial times in Dodgson's life. Hence, the possibility of a zealous family member trying to hide from posterity Dodgson's faults cannot be totally ruled out.

When editing the text, I have used the same conventions as appear in the first volume. Some minor silent corrections have been made to Dodgson's text, but otherwise it is reproduced as written. Dodgson makes more use of initials for family members. I have written the names out in full for the ease of readers. When Dodgson uses the left-hand side of the page, normally kept blank, he does so to supplement entries, often at a later date. These are indicated by square brackets; [ ]. On the rare occasion that Dodgson uses square brackets within his text, I have silently changed these to round brackets; ( ). For additions which I have made to Dodgson's text, for example when a word has been omitted, I have used { }.

I have used the following short titles which appear in footnotes:

Collingwood	*The Life and Letters of Lewis Carroll* (T. Fisher Unwin: 1898)
Diary 1	*Lewis Carroll's Diaries: Volume 1* edited by Edward Wakeling (Lewis Carroll Society: 1993)
Gernsheim	*Lewis Carroll, Photographer* (Max Parrish: 1949)
Handbook	*The Lewis Carroll Handbook* edited by Williams, Madan and Green, revised by Denis Crutch (Dawson: 1979)
Jabberwocky	The Journal of the Lewis Carroll Society
Letters	*The Letters of Lewis Carroll* edited by Morton N. Cohen with the assistance of Roger Lancelyn Green (Macmillan: 1979)

Library	*Lewis Carroll's Library* edited by Jeffrey Stern (Lewis Carroll Society of North America: 1981)
Oxford Pamphlets	*The Oxford Pamphlets, Leaflets, and Circulars of Charles Lutwidge Dodgson* edited by Edward Wakeling (University Press of Virginia: 1993)

Again, I acknowledge with grateful thanks a number of people who have helped me with this volume of Dodgson's journal, but I single out two people in particular who have helped me in the task of providing detailed footnotes. Ann Fell, from the Cleveland Family History Society, has provided me with comprehensive notes on many people mentioned by Dodgson in his journal. This has been an enormous task requiring visits to various parts of the country to check local records. She has carefully researched the census records of 1851 and 1861 to provide family details. Her efforts have made it possible to identify nearly everyone, even of a casual acquaintance, mentioned in this journal. My second major support has come from Stanley Chapman. He spent many hours in the Public Records Office and other dark and dreary places searching out answers to my many questions. His tenacity uncovered details of Dodgson's London acquaintances and some interesting supplementary material on engravers, artists, musicians, and contemporary news items. Others who have supported me in many ways include Anne Clark Amor, Morton Cohen, Selwyn Goodacre, Kazumi Goto, Richard Lancelyn Green, Peter Harries, Margaret Heaton, Iris Henson, Veronica Hickie, Janet McMullen, Mark Richards, Celia Salisbury Jones and John Wing. The project is made possible by the generosity and encouragement of the Senior Trustee of the C. L. Dodgson Estate, Mr. Philip Dodgson Jaques, to whom I am indebted.

Edward Wakeling

The Private Journal of Charles Lutwidge Dodgson

JOURNAL NUMBER 4

Diary for the year 1856
January to December

Jan: 1. (Tu). At Croft - walked up to the castle on a farewell visit, and borrowed some *Art Journals*, which contain a most abusive notice of Ruskin's *Notes on the Royal Academy*.[1]

Jan: 2. (W). Dined with Mr. John Chaytor, the first time I ever did such a thing.[2] I met Mr.

---

1. *Notes on some of the principal pictures exhibited in the rooms of the Royal Academy (and the Society of Painters in Water Colours)* by John Ruskin, was published in 1855. Ruskin (1819-1900) was a Gentleman Commoner at Christ Church and Slade Professor of Art 1869-79 and 1883-84. As an author and artist he was an influential critic and reformer. He championed the cause of the Pre-Raphaelites. *The Art Journal* for August 1855 (No. VIII) contained an anonymous article titled "Mr. Ruskin's 'Notes' on 'The Exhibition'" in which the writer claims that "there is no sign of any useful study in anything that he [Ruskin] has written" and goes on to state "that if he knew enough of Art, he would mention in his way young painters who gave forth promise of future distinction; but so much cannot be expected of him." The writer accuses Ruskin of "scurrility," "arrogance," "flippancy" and "ignorance of Art."

2. John Clervaux Chaytor (1806-94), second son of Sir William Chaytor of Croft, Bart., and his wife Isabella; educated at Worcester College, Oxford, B.A. 1829, M.A. 1831, Barrister Inner Temple 1832. He married Lydia Frances Brown in 1824. There were eleven children. Chaytor was a landowner and farmer at Croft who took an active interest in the business and social life of the area. Dodgson's first opportunity to dine with

and the younger Mrs. Johnson, and Mr. Simpson.[3] I enjoyed the party better than I expected.

Jan: 3. (Th).   The party left Croft about one, and arrived in Ripon about three. George Longley is ordered off to the Crimea again, and leaves here tomorrow.[4] As there is no man-servant at present, I am housed in the Residence, instead of being turned out as before into lodgings. Went on with *Alton Locke*, a powerful, and grandly-written book.[5]

Chaytor probably stems from the poor relations which existed between Sir William Chaytor and Dodgson's father. Sir William disagreed with the building, design, management and trusteeship of the new school at Croft established by Archdeacon Dodgson soon after taking up his position as Rector. Acrimonious correspondence survives between the two men mainly concerning the Chaytor pew in the church [Papers of Sir William Chaytor, North Yorkshire County Record Office].

3.   William Johnson (1794-1875), a farmer of Stapleton in the parish of Croft, together with his wife Elizabeth, almost twenty years his junior. John Simpson (1790-1870), another local farmer (Lodge Farm, Halnaby) who was for many years churchwarden at Croft.

4.   George Longley (1835-92), second son of Charles Thomas Longley (1794-1868), Bishop of Ripon, and his wife Caroline Sophia. At this time, Longley was a commissioned officer, with the local rank of Captain, in the Turkish Contingent Engineers, and for his services in the Crimea was awarded the Turkish Medal. He joined the Army in 1853; Lieut. 1854; Capt. 1859; Major 1861; Lieut.-Col. Royal Engineers 1872.

5.   Charles Kingsley (1819-75) published his first novel, *Alton Locke, Tailor and Poet. An Autobiography*, in 1850.

Jan: 5. (Sat).　I find in the memoirs of C. Matthews {sic}, which I have taken out of the Library here, a curious theatrical custom, that in *Henry VIII* the character of Bishop Gardiner should be acted by the principal comedian of the company: (Meadows acted it when I saw the play at the Princess', which rather surprised me at the time).[6]

Jan: 7. (M).　Received from the Palace an invitation to dinner for Tuesday the 15th, which I declined, as I hope to be in London by then.[7] [I also got an invitation, (which followed me to London,) to dine at Richmond on that day, and stay the night.] Lent *Maud*[8] to Miss Erskine, who

---

6.　Charles Mathews (1776-1835), an English actor and entertainer renowned for his imitations of numerous well-known characters of his age. His *Memoirs* were actually written by his second wife. Dodgson first saw *Henry VIII* at the Princess's Theatre, London, on 22 June 1855.

7.　The Bishop's Palace at Ripon, home of Charles Thomas Longley (1794-1868), Bishop of Ripon, and his family. Longley was a Student at Christ Church 1812-28, gained his B.A. in 1815, M.A. in 1818, B. & D.D. in 1829. He was Greek Reader in 1822, tutor and censor in 1825-8, elected proctor in 1827, and honorary Student in 1867-8. He was rector of Tytherley, Hampshire, in 1827, headmaster of Harrow from 1829 before becoming Bishop of Ripon in 1836. He went on to become Archbishop of York in 1860 and eventually Archbishop of Canterbury in 1862 until his death. Dodgson went to school with the eldest son, Henry Longley (1833-99). After Rugby, both matriculated at Christ Church.

8.　Tennyson's *Maud, and other Poems* was published in 1855.

1856

called.[9] The Bishop called in the afternoon, with Fanny Longley, Caroline, and Rosamond.[10] Finished *Alton Locke*.

He tells the tale well of the privations and miseries of the poor, but I wish he would propose some more definite remedy, and especially that he would tell us what he wishes to substitute for the iniquitous "sweating" system in tailoring and other trades.

Kingsley's arguments in favour of miracles are much inferior to Paley's, I think: one instance that he adduces of what we ought never to expect to see worked, *viz*: that an amputated member should grow again, we find actually done in the case of Malchus, nor is such a cure (when time is allowed for it) beyond the powers of Science.[11]

---

9. Harriet Frances Erskine (born c.1814) was the eldest daughter of the Very Rev. Henry David Erskine, Dean of Ripon. A portrait of Dean Erskine is in an album of Dodgson's photographs at Princeton University Library.

10. Dodgson knew the Bishop's daughters well, and the following year he wrote "The Legend of Scotland" for them. The daughters were Mary Henrietta (born c.1837), Frances "Fanny" Elizabeth (born c.1840), Caroline Georgiana (1843-67), and Rosamond Esther Harriet (born c.1844).

11. *The Works of William Paley*, published in 1819 with numerous reprints, contained the collected papers of William Paley (1743-1805), Archdeacon of Carlisle, on such subjects as the evidences of Christianity, moral and political philosophy, natural theology and scriptural history.

[Tyrwhitt says he does not mean "attach itself again," but actually *grow* again like a plant. I never noticed this *naturalness* of miracles before. Some of the modern Romish miracles are thus *contra naturam* not merely *supra naturem*.][12]

If the book were but a little more definite, it might stir up many fellow-workers in the same good field of social improvement. Oh that God, in his good providence, may make me hereafter such a worker! But alas what are the means! Each has his *nostrum* to propound, and in the Babel of voices nothing is done. I would thankfully spend and be spent so long as I were sure of really effecting something by the sacrifice, and not merely lying down under the wheels of some irresistible Juggernaut.

---

12.   Richard St. John Tyrwhitt (1827-95), Student of Christ Church, a poet and writer of many books including *Hugh Heron Ch. Ch.* and *A Handbook of Pictorial Art* (1866). He was an artist of note exhibiting at the Royal Academy. Dodgson photographed a number of Tyrwhitt's etchings. For a photograph of Tyrwhitt by Dodgson, see *Oxford Pamphlets*, p. 178. The two men often discussed social and religious matters, in this case the feasibility of unnatural and super-natural events which might be deemed as miracles. Tyrwhitt was from an ancient Northumberland family descended from Sir Hercules Archil Tyrwhitt living in 1067. His father was recorder of Chester living at Nantyr Hall. Richard St. John Tyrwhitt married Eliza-Anne Stanhope in 1858 and they had one son. His wife died just over a year after their marriage. He remarried in 1861. His second wife, Caroline Yorke, produced six children.

That is a wild and beautiful bit of poetry, the song of "Call the cattle home." I remember hearing it sung at Albrighton: I wonder if any one there could have entered into the spirit of *Alton Locke*.[13] I think not. I think the character of most that I meet with is merely refined animal, viewing life either as βιος απολανστικος merely, or intellectually.[14] How few seem to care for the only subjects of real interest in life. What am I to say so? Am *I* a deep philosopher, or a great genius? I think neither. What talents I have, I desire to devote to His service, and may he purify me, and take away my pride and selfishness. Oh that *I* might hear "Well done, good and faithful servant"!

Jan: 8. (Tu). Re-wrote a sonnet for the beginning of Mary's volume of manuscript Poetry, which I finished after midnight last night.[15] Got the first number of *The Train*: it is, I think, only average in talent, and an intense imitation of Dickens throughout. I don't think it has *any* chance

---

13. There are two Albrighton's in England; one near Shrewsbury, the other just north-west of Wolverhampton. The one Dodgson visited is unknown.

14. The Greek, from Aristotle, translates: "a life devoted to enjoyment."

15. The sonnet and his sister's poetry volume do not appear to have survived.

of surviving the year.[16]

Jan: 9. (W). Mr. Jameson paid me a call.[17] In the course of the day Mrs. Wood (the new resident at Hollin Hall, along the Harrogate road) called (with two children, Albert and Rosa): they promise to be pleasant acquaintances.[18] Sent my sonnet to Menella to be corrected and criticised.[19]

Jan: 10. (Th). Sent a copy of the "Palace of Humbug" to

---

16. Dodgson's forecast was almost right; *The Train*, edited by Edmund Yates, lasted until June 1858. Dodgson contributed eight items to this monthly magazine (see n. *104* below). Issues were bound in half-annual volumes. Dodgson's comparison with Dickens is probably a reference to *Household Words* a highly popular weekly magazine which Dickens edited from 1850 to 1859.

17. Joseph Jameson (c.1794-1875), admitted Trinity, Cambridge, 1820; ordained deacon York 1816; priest 1817; curate Harpham, Yorks. 1817-21; precentor & minor canon Ripon Cathedral 1821-75; perpetual curate Cleasby, Yorks. 1826-75, married Nancy Matilda Wood Schaak in 1825. He had family and friendship links with the Wood family of Hollin Hall, Ripon.

18. Mrs. Charlotte Augusta Wood (1821?-61) was married to Frederick Henry Wood (1811-86) and they had three children; Albert Charles (1841-90), Eliza Rose (1843-?) and Henry Richard Hugh (1847-83). Mr. Wood, a land-owner and magistrate, lived at the family home of Hollin Hall inherited from his father, Henry Richard Wood (1786-1844). Dodgson's remarks that Mrs. Wood had only recently moved to Hollin Hall suggests that she lived elsewhere for some of her married life,. This is supported by the fact that the eldest son was born in York.

19. Menella Bute Smedley (1820-77). See *Diary 1*, p. 107 n. *121*.

Mr. Yates, on the chance of the first not having reached him through Frank Smedley.[20] Dined at the Griffiths.[21] Young Scholfield of Fairlawn, a Cambridge man, called on me in the morning.[22]

Jan: 11. (F). Went with my father, aunt, Fanny, and Elizabeth, to an evening party at the Miss Woods: the evening was a very pleasant one.[23] I met both Mr. and Mrs. Wood of Skelton there, and learnt from Mr. Wood

---

20. Dodgson's humorous poem, "The Palace of Humbug" was refused by Edmund Yates for both *The Comic Times* and *The Train*. It was also turned down by *Punch*, but finally saw publication in *The Oxford Critic*, number 1, dated 29 May 1857. Dodgson copied it into *Mischmasch*. Frank Smedley was his cousin; see *Diary 1*, p. 110 n. *127*.

21. James Griffith (1797-?), educated at Durham School; B.A. Durham 1816; admitted Grays Inn as barrister 1824, moved to Ripon with his young wife, Katherine, nearly thirty years his junior, sometime before 1851. The children were Katherine (born 1850), John Charles (born 1852) and Mary Frances (born 1853).

22. The Cambridge scholar is possibly Charles Richard Scholfield (1832-1902), admitted Trinity 1850; B.A. 1855; M.A. 1858; ordained deacon 1857; priest 1858; after several curacies became vicar of Gt. Ouseburn, Yorks. 1868-89. He was the son of William Freer Scholfield and Mary née Champion. The Yorkshire Directory (1857) lists F. W. Scholfield as living at Fairlawn, in the village of Sharow, which is near to Ripon. Transposition errors in directories are common.

23. The Miss Woods, Louisa Frances (1784-1868) and Emma Juliana (1798-1885), were members of the Boynton Wood family of Hollin Hall and aunts of the current resident, Frederick Henry Wood. They lived at Borrage Terrace, Ripon.

that my correspondence on the subject of Mr. Eckersall had produced most satisfactory results.[24] He succeeded in clearing his friend's character, and Mrs. Wood, who joined him there, became acquainted with Mrs. Bainbridge's mother, Mrs. Palmer, and with her sister, Mrs. Pickard, and they are now the greatest of friends. They tell me also that Mr. Bainbridge has just returned from the sea.[25]

---

24.   The Woods of Skelton were Edward Wood (1796-1875) and his wife, Charlotte. Mr. Wood was educated at Trinity, Cambridge; B.A. 1819; ordained priest 1821; curate St Agnes 1819, St Austell 1820, Wheldrake, Yorks. 1827; perpetual curate Skelton on Ure 1833 until his death. Edward Wood was cousin to Frederick Wood's father, Henry Richard Wood, who in turn was brother-in-law to Rev. Charles Eckersall (1797-1863). For Dodgson's correspondence on Mr. Eckersall, see *Diary 1*, pp. 95, 96 & 100.

25.   Lieutenant Henry Bainbridge R.N. (1816-77) and his wife Mary Agnes (b. 1811) lived at 19 St. Hilda's Terrace, Ruswarp, Whitby, and not at 5 East Terrace as suggested in *Diary 1*, p. 54 n. *13*. Dodgson became acquainted with the family during his stay in Whitby in 1854. There were two daughters, Florence Hilda (b. 1848) and Agnes Constance (b. 1850). Also residing with the family was a nephew, George Henry S. Bainbridge (b. 1840) and a niece, Isabella M. A. Campbell (b. 1833). Mrs. Bainbridge's parents, Lieutenant Colonel Bissel Harvey and his wife Mary, also lived with them. Dodgson used the Bainbridge home as a location for his photographic equipment during the summer of 1856; see 29 September. In the diary entry, Dodgson suggests that Mrs. Palmer is the mother of Mrs. Bainbridge, but this is not the case. The entry also suggests that Mrs. Pickard was Mrs. Bainbridge's sister although the family link has not been proved (see n. *173* below). Henry Bainbridge was promoted to Lieutenant in 1845. He was with the Coast Guard Service at Whitby in 1850-2. In 1855, he was attached to the Transport Service in the Crimea (see 12 July, below).

1856

Was saved the walk back by Mr. Griffith giving me a seat in his fly.

Jan: 12. (Sat). I called on the Griffiths alone in the morning, and found Mr. Griffith at home. Thence with Mary and Louisa to call on the Miss Woods, who were out. Fell in with the little Griffiths on the way. Fanny, Elizabeth, and I spent an exceedingly pleasant evening with the Scholfields, where we met Mr. and Mrs. Gray.[26] Mrs. Scholfield has a copy of the *Madonna della Seggiola*, the size of the original, and framed in imitation of it: the picture is circular, so that all without the circle, (in Baxter's oblong copy and others,) must be the addition of a later hand.[27] I took a copy of a very good shadow-picture of Louis Napoleon, which

---

26. Edmund Gray (1826-90), educated at Durham University; B.A. 1848; M.A. 1851; ordained priest 1850; curate Dacre, Yorks. 1849-52; incumbent at Sharow 1852-84; rector at West Rounton 1884 until his death. Author of *Lessons on the Book of Common Prayer* (1862) and *Notes and Questions on the Epistles for Sundays in the Christian Year*. Mary Gray (1825-91) was his wife, but there do not appear to be any children from the marriage.

27. Raphael's *Madonna della Seggiola* (The Madonna of the Chair) is a circular picture in the Gallery Pitti, Florence. George Baxter (1804-67), a wood-engraver, born at Lewes but went to London in 1827 where he became famous for his engraving and new method of printing in oil-colours. His work became known as "Baxter prints.".

1856

they had brought from Paris.[28] There too I met with a copy of that lithograph from Lawrence I have been trying to get. It is called "The lovely sisters," engraved by Lewis, and published by Boys.[29] [see May 10]

[I met with a curious anecdote in Mary Howitt's *Sketches of a Literary Life*.[30] The house of Professor Longfellow at Cambridge was once the head-quarters of Washington. One night the poet, looking from his window, saw a figure ride by in the dim star-light: the face he could not distinguish, but the cocked hat, tall erect

---

28.   Probably Charles Louis Napoleon III (1808-73), Emperor of the French, nephew of Napoleon Bonaparte. His foreign policy resulted in the participation of the French in the Crimean War.

29.   "The Calmady Children" by Sir Thomas Lawrence (1769-1830), engraved by Frederick Christian Lewis (1779-1856). Lawrence was a portrait artist elected to the Royal Academy in 1794, and chosen President in 1820. His portraits of leading Regency figures and notable European dignitaries were fashionable at the time. Lewis was an engraver and landscape painter renowned for his engravings of Lawrence's portraits produced in the stipple manner. He sketched from nature around Enfield and in Devon, exhibiting landscapes at the Water-Colour Society, the British Institution, and the Royal Academy. See 10 May, below.

30.   Possibly *My own Story; or, the Autobiography of a child* by Mary Howitt (London: 1845) or *The Author's Daughter* (London: 1845). The title, *Sketches of a Literary Life*, has not been identified. Mary Botham Howitt (179?-1888) was born in Uttoxeter. She was a Quaker and married William Howitt, also a Quaker and writer, in 1831. She was the author of "Will you walk into my parlour?" said the spider to the fly, parodied by Dodgson as "Will you walk a little faster?" She became a Roman Catholic and died in Rome.

1856

figure, and often-described white horse, were all there. The horseman passed the house, returned, passed again, and then was no more seen. The narrator of this was a firm believer in its "spiritual" interpretation.]

Jan: 14. (M).   Accompanied a party to York to visit Mr. King, also to Museum, etc. I saw in a shop window a coloured print after a new (?) picture of Burraud {sic}, (painter of the Chorister (?)), a very beautiful one: the subject is "Evangeline." [31]

Jan: 15. (Tu).   Left Ripon for London at 8.58 and reached town 9.30 in time to dine with Uncle Skeffington.

Jan: 16. (W).   Called on Uncle Hassard in the temple, and arranged to go with himself and Percy to the Haymarket tomorrow. He

---

31.   Henry Barraud (1812-74) excelled as an animal painter. Many of his later pictures were engraved and became very popular. His brother, William (1810-50) was also an artist of note, painting chiefly horses and dogs. Both brothers were joint exhibitors at the Royal Academy and the British Institution. Henry Barraud's "Evangeline" was exhibited at the British Institution in 1855 and is based on a line from Longfellow's poem, *Evangeline, A Tale of Acadie* (1847): "Yet were her thoughts of him, and at times a feeling of sadness" (First Part, Canto III, line 109). In 1713, Acadia (now known as Nova Scotia) was ceded to Britain from the French. Some time after, the inhabitants were removed from their homes and sent to other far-off colonies. The poem is descriptive of the fate of some of these unfortunate people.

1856

tells me that Frank is trying to get into the artillery: the examination begins on Monday: and that he has applied to Lord Hardinge for an Infantry commission for Percy.[32] Went to the Photographic Exhibition: there is a very beautiful historical picture by Lake Price, called "the scene in the tower," taken from life.[33] It is a capital idea for making up pictures. There is another, nearly as good, of the same kind, "the confessional." Some of the coloured portraits are exquisite - equal to the best enamel: one of the best of the portraits is Kean, in the character of Cardinal Wolsey.[34]

---

32. Dodgson's two cousins, Francis "Frank" Hume (1834-1917) and Percy (1838-86) were sons of Uncle Hassard Hume Dodgson; see *Diary 1*, p. 106 n. *120*. Following success in the Woolwich entrance examination for army officers, Frank Dodgson trained and later in the year became a lieutenant in the Royal Artillery, a position he held until 1864. Viscount Henry Hardinge (1785-1856) was Chief Secretary for Ireland in 1830 and again in 1834-5. He was Governor General of India from 1844 to 1847. From 1852 he was Commander-in-Chief of the British Army. He died on 24 September 1856.

33. William Lake Price (c.1810-96), a water-colourist, who turned photographer. His work was patronized by Prince Albert.

34. Dodgson saw Charles Kean (1811-68) in the role of Cardinal Wolsey when he attended a production of *Henry VIII* at the Princess's Theatre on 22 June 1855; see *Diary 1*, p. 105. Kean was manager of the Princess's Theatre from 1851 to 1859 during which he embellished historical drama with lavish spectacle. His portrayal of Shakespearean characters brought him great fame.

1856

Called on Southey, and asked him to come over on Friday for a photographic day: I went also to Wimpole Street but Mayo was out.[35]

In the evening I went to the Princess' and had five hours of unmixed enjoyment. Firstly, *Hamlet*, with Kean as Hamlet, Walter Lacy as ghost, and Miss Heath as Ophelia.[36] Kean was best in the play scene (evidently grouped from Maclise's picture) but the part did not suit him nearly as well as Cardinal Wolsey.[37]

---

35.   Reginald Southey (1835-99); see *Diary 1*, p. 66 n. *50*. Robert Mayo (1832-?); see *Diary 1*, p. 77 n. *74*. Robert Mayo was the second son of Thomas Mayo (1790-1871), President of the Royal College of Physicians, who resided at 56 Wimpole Street.

36.   Walter Lacy (1809-?) made his debut on the London stage at the Haymarket Theatre in 1838 in the role of Charles Surface in *School for Scandal*. In 1852 he joined Charles Kean at the Princess's Theatre where he remained in the company for seven years being much acclaimed for his acting abilities. He became Professor of Elocution at the Royal Academy of Music, a post he held for 16 years. Caroline Heath (Mrs. Wilson Barrett) made her professional debut at the Princess's Theatre in 1852 in the character of Stella, the heroine of Boucicault's *The Prima Donna*. She remained with the company for several years playing in various Shakespearean revivals, including the role of Anne Boleyn in *Henry VIII* in 1855, seen by Dodgson on 22 June.

37.   Daniel Maclise R.A. (1806-70), the son of a well-to-do Irish artisan, moved to London in 1827 in order to enter the Royal Academy Schools. He contributed nearly eighty caricatures to *Fraser's Magazine* between 1830-6. His strongly developed historical imagination resulted in paintings of scenes in Tudor and Jacobean times. He also produced several distinctive Shakespearean pictures. He painted a number of frescoes in the House of Lords.

1856

The madness of Ophelia was beautifully acted: I think the scene "I would give you violets, but they withered all when my father died" must have been grouped from H. O'Brien's picture.[38] The evening concluded with *The Maid and the Magpie, or the Fairy Paradisa and Hanky Panky the enchanter.*[39] The scenery was gorgeous almost beyond description, and some of the buffoonery amusing, but the tricks etc. required a more juvenile spectator.

Some really wonderful performing dogs were introduced: one of the most curious of their tricks was standing on a barrel and, by shifting the feet, rolling it backwards up a ladder: the dogs seemed to enjoy it as much as the audience.

The concluding scene, where the dance in *Henry VIII* is acted in dumb show entirely by children, was the prettiest thing I ever saw on the stage, and the pretty little Anne Boleyn went through her part in a manner quite worthy

---

38. H. O'Brien is not identified.

39. *The Maid and The Magpie* was by the American actor and dramatist, John W. Howard Payne (1791-1852). Written in 1815, it was frequently re-staged, revised and rewritten by subsequent dramatists.

of an older actor. The little queen Catherine (A. Smith) was a merry little creature of about five years old, and pulled the ears of Anne Boleyn (Emily Edmonds) in anything but a malicious spirit. These little creatures enacted a second transformation, and Henry VIII became a tiny Harlequin, with Anne Boleyn as Columbine. The whole scene was a picture not to be forgotten.[40]

Jan: 17. (Th). Consulted Mr. Bowman, the oculist, about my right eye:[41] he does not seem to think anything can be done to remedy it, but recommends me not to read long at a time, nor on the railway, and to keep to large type by candlelight. I then got a ticket at Colnaghis' for the Dulwich Gallery,[42] but not having time to get there today, went again to the Photographic

---

40.   The actresses, A. Smith and Emily Edmonds, are not identified.

41.   The nature of Dodgson's sight problems are not known. The consultant, Mr. Bowman, later Sir William Bowman (1816-92), was a renowned ophthalmic surgeon. In later life, Dodgson suffered mild attacks of migraine which temporarily affected his sight. He saw "moving fortifications" and experienced blind spots.

42.   Dominic Colnaghi (1790-1879) and Martin Colnaghi (1821-1908), uncle and nephew, were art dealers with a European reputation working for the firm founded by Paul Colnaghi, the father of Dominic. They had connections with a number of major art galleries in London, including the Marlborough Gallery in Pall Mall.

gallery. The picture of "the monk," (which I missed in the first visit), is magnificent.

Thence I went down to Putney, which I reached about three. None of the family but Percy seem to have grown at all since I last saw them and poor little Charlotte is even more stunted and dwarfed-looking, as her face gets older; with a sweet sad expression it is almost painful to see. Percy and I came to town by omnibus and went with Uncle Hassard to the Haymarket.

First we had *The Little Treasure* by Miss Blanche Fane etc., she is very young and acted with amazing spirit.[43] A great objection to such plays is the insult they offer to human nature by simulating its noblest passions, those which redeem it from mere sensual brute life. It is a profanation of things we should rather revere.

The pantomime *The Butterfly's Ball and the Grasshopper's feast, or Harlequin and the Genius of Spring* was very good, and some of the scenery as gorgeous as the Princess'. The evening concluded with *Only a Halfpenny*, which

---

43. *The Little Treasure*, by Augustus Glossop Harris (1825-73), actor, manager and dramatist. Blanche Fane is not identified.

was amusing, but, like *The Little Treasure*, rather too much spun out in parts.[44]

Jan: 18. (F). Southey came over to spend the day in photography, but we went instead to Dr. Diamond of the Surrey Lunatic Asylum: he gave me two he has done lately, an excellent full length of Uncle Skeffington, and a boy at King's College, Frank Forester.[45]

In the evening the Putney party including Charlotte and Amy, came to dinner in Brompton.

Jan: 19. (Sat). Went over to Putney and stayed for dinner, and thence to Oxford, calling in Brompton on the way.

Hilary Term 1856

Jan: 19. (Sat). Got to Ch. Ch. about half past ten, and

44. *Harlequin and The Little Glass Slipper, The Magic Pumpkin, and The Butterflies Ball and Grasshopper's Feast,* a grand pantomime by Edward Leman Blanchard (1820-89). *Only a Halfpenny,* by John Oxenford (1812-77) translator of outstanding merit, author of nearly a hundred plays, and for over twenty-five years dramatic critic to *The Times*.

45. Dr. Hugh Welch Diamond (1809-86) resident superintendent of female patients at Surrey County Asylum, became secretary to the London Photographic Society in 1853, and is said to have invented the paper or cardboard photographic process. Frank Forester has not been identified.

had tea with Liddon.[46]

Jan: 20. (Sun). St. Aldates in the morning with Mayo. St. Paul's in the evening with Liddon.

Jan: 21. (M). Called on the Dean, and got his consent to arrange the public lectures as I find best. We also discussed Frank's case: the Dean does not seem to like the idea of his holding the studentship and at the same time trying for a military commission: however the question of leave of absence need not be finally settled till the result of the present Examination is known.[47]

Attended the tutors' meeting to settle lectures from the term, but as I find it necessary to see the men personally before all can be arranged, I have sent round a notice in Hall, the first I have issued as Mathematical lecturer, requesting them to attend in the lecture room at 10 tomorrow. Walked with Southey in the afternoon.

---

46. Henry Parry Liddon (1829-90); see *Diary 1*, p. 89 n. *93*.

47. There was obviously a problem with Frank Dodgson's attempt at a commission with the Royal Artillery (to serve in the Crimea) and at the same time holding his Westminster Studentship at Christ Church. A decision was delayed until Frank's success in the Woolwich examination was known on 9 March. He chose to remain at Christ Church until the summer, joining trainee officers at Woolwich in the autumn. He kept his Studentship until 1857. See n. *32* above.

1856

Began "Novelty and Romancement, a broken spell," for the *Train*.[48] [Sep. 12]

Jan: 22. (Tu). Of the 60 men sent for, only 23 appeared: I have sent for the rest to my rooms.

Wrote to ask Uncle Skeffington to get me a photographic apparatus, as I want some occupation here than mere reading and writing.[49] Lunch and walked with Fowler of Lincoln.[50]

I am thinking of beginning a sort of day-book for entering *everything* in, another private one, and gradually form special books. However I shall begin the thing on paper.[51]

Drew up various books connected with the Mathematical Lecture.[52]

---

48.   "Novelty and Romancement. A Broken Spell." See n. *104* below.

49.   Dodgson obtained his own photographic camera with the guidance of his colleague, Reginald Southey. See 17, 18 March and 1 May below. Uncle Skeffington, his mother's unmarried brother, owned a wet-plate camera, and he may have suggested to Dodgson a photographic dealer in London, Ottewill's of Charlotte Street, who manufactured cameras to order. Dodgson assisted Uncle Skeffington on a photographic expedition to Richmond on 8 September 1856 (see *Diary 1*, p. 130).

50.   Thomas Fowler (1832-1904); see *Diary 1*, p. 64 n. *41*.

51.   The day-book has not survived.

52.   The book recording his mathematical lectures has not survived.

Jan: 23. (W).   Breakfasted with Prout.[53]

My second notice in Hall produced no more men: I have sent for them now individually.

Jan: 24. (Th).   Called on the Dean to consult him on various questions connected with the lecture. We settled:

First, that those men who undertake to get up their work by themselves may do so, and are to be examined from time to time during term.

Second, that a man need only get up in the term a proportional part of his work, according to the time he means to go in. When the lecture has reached that point [or "when *he* has reached the point," will be a better rule, and encourage them to work hard] he may cease attending.

Third, that help may be given in Arithmetic to such as really need it.

Fourth, that the idle are to be at once reported to the Dean.

---

53.   Thomas Jones Prout (1823-1909), Senior Student at Christ Church, who in 1865 headed the committee of Students who contested the absolute rule of the Dean and Chapter. Their actions were successful, and Prout became known as "The Man who Slew the Canons." Prout, born in Edinburgh, was a Westminster scholar who entered Christ Church in 1842, took his B.A. in 1846 and was a tutor for ten years from 1851. He was elected censor 1857-61 and proctor in 1859. He was also vicar of Binsey from 1857 until 1891. For further details, and for a photograph of Prout, see *Oxford Pamphlets*, pp. 12-13.

Jan: 25. (F).   Called on Price, to ask his advice on the order in which men should read their subjects for Moderations.[54] He gave me the list opposite. [Arithmetic
Euclid 3 books.
Algebra first part.
Euclid books 4, 5, 6.
Trigonometry plane.
Algebra second part.
Salmon 13 chapters.
Diff: Cal: all but three dimensions.
Int: Cal:
Spherical Trigonometry.]
His way of teaching *Euclid* is to make the men write it out: I am inclined to try the plan.

I sent for the rest of the men to come to me this evening, and got all, except those who have not yet come up, of whom there are eight.

Jan: 26. (Sat).   One lecture in Trigonometry and the first this term. Sent *Tasso, Herbert* etc. to be bound.[55]

---

54.   Professor Bartholomew "Bat" Price (1818-98); see *Diary 1*, p. 57 n. 22. Moderations were the second set of examinations prior to gaining a degree.

55.   Dodgson had two volumes of *Tasso* in Italian bound in vellum and another copy from the series of *Pickering's Diamond Classics* (dated 1822) in his library, together with a copy of *Herbert's Poems* (see *Library*, p. 21 lots 394, 401 and p. 25 lot 476).

1856

Jan: 28. (M). Gave my two first lectures in the lecture room, nine men at the *Euclid*, eleven at the Algebra lecture (there ought to have been twelve at each). Harwood came in the evening to ask not to join the Euclid lecture. I have two other volunteers (in the Algebra lecture), Pusey and Bowman. Examined Gregory, in the vacation work set him by Lloyd: he knew nothing of it - he makes the fourth I have examined for him, and whom he has then reported to the Dean, (the other three were Gordon, Irvine, and Fergusson).[56]

---

56.   Thomas Eustace Harwood matriculated at Christ Church on 16 October 1855, aged 18, and gained his B.A. in 1859. He took his M.A. in 1862 and held various curacies between 1860 and 1876 until becoming vicar of Old Windsor. Henry Bouverie Pusey matriculated at Christ Church on 31 May 1855, aged 18, and gained his B.A. in 1860. He took his M.A. in 1862. He became a lieutenant with the 76th Foot, and died at sea in 1869. Charles Henry Bowman matriculated at Christ Church on 18 October 1854, aged 19. He was a servitor in 1854 and gained his B.A. in 1858. He went on to become vicar of Llanfair-Waterdine, Radnor, in 1885. Francis Hood Gregory matriculated at Christ Church on 18 October 1854, aged 17, and gained his B.A. in 1860. He took his M.A. in 1865 and became a major in the 15th Hussars. Arthur Pitman Gordon matriculated at Christ Church on 31 May 1855, aged 18, and gained his B.A. in 1859. He took his M.A. in 1862 and became rector of Newtimber, Sussex, in 1863. John William Irvine matriculated at Christ Church on 30 May 1855, aged 19, and gained his B.A. in 1859. He took his M.A. in 1864 and became assistant-master at Charterhouse from 1859-64. From 1870 he was rector of St. Mary-at-the-Walls, Colchester. He died on 16 July 1906. James Ranken Fergusson, later Sir, matriculated at Christ Church on 31 May 1855, aged 19, and succeeded to 2nd baronet after the death of his father, Sir William Fergusson of Edinburgh. In 1858, he became a barrister-at-law at Lincoln's Inn. Gregory's vacation work was set by Charles Lloyd (1824-62), tutor at Christ Church who shared some of the mathematical teaching with Dodgson (see *Diary 1*, p. 132 n. *165*).

Jan: 29. (Tu). Breakfasted with Swabey, to arrange about teaching in his school.[57] We settled that I am to come at ten on Sunday, and at two on Tuesdays and Fridays to teach sums. I gave the first lesson there today, to a class of 8 boys, and found it much more pleasant than I expected. The contrast is very striking between town and country boys: here they are sharp, boisterous, and in the highest spirits, the difficulty of teaching being not to get an answer, but to prevent all answering at once. They seem tractable and in good order.

[Mayhew, Charles (a teacher).

2. Roberts, William.

5. West, George.

7. Payne, George.

3. Simpson, Charles.

4. Smith, Henry.

1. Daw, William.

6. Stone, Henry.]

I stayed a short time afterwards to watch: for want of teachers, the master had to conduct two lessons at once, while a third (a writing lesson) went on by itself.

---

57. Henry Swabey (1826-78), rector of St. Aldates, formerly an undergraduate at Pembroke College where he took his B.A. in 1848 and his M.A. in 1851. He became rector of St. Aldates (opposite Tom Gate, Christ Church) in 1850. He was secretary of The Society for the Promotion of Christian Knowledge from 1863 until his death.

1856

Collyns has come up for a few days, and is trying to get his name replaced on the books here.[58]

In the evening we asked the table of Bachelors to Common Room (I taking Rocke).[59]

In future I shall record all matters connected with the Mathematical Lecture in a separate book.[60]

[I think it would be a very good idea to have the slides of a magic lantern painted to represent characters in some play, which might be read aloud, a sort of Marionette performance.][61]

Jan: 30. (W). There was a meeting in Common Room of student-masters in the evening, as we had been invited by the Commission[62] to

---

58. John Martyn Collyns (1827-1912); see *Diary 1*, p. 65 n. *44*.

59. Alfred Beale Rocke (1833-87); see *Diary 1*, p. 84 n. *88*.

60. Record of mathematical lectures; see n. *52* above.

61. For more on Dodgson's interest in marionettes, see *Diary 1*, pp. 81-2, 110-11. Dodgson subsequently purchased a magic lantern with which he entertained the children at Croft School. See 31 December below.

62. At this time there were no Statutes governing the management and organisation of Christ Church, a situation unchallenged for over 300 years. In 1858, a Commission put forward a series of recommendations following discussions with the academic staff. This summoned up a wind of change which culminated in *The Christ Church, Oxford, Act of 1867*. For more details, see *Oxford Pamphlets*, pp. 12, 62-65.

lay propositions before them: we decided on not taking the initiative, but offering to discuss any matter they chose to lay before us.

Jan: 31. (Th). Collyns got his name put on the books here again.

Feb: 1. (F). The master at St. Aldates school asked if I would join the first class of girls with the boys. I tried it for today, but I do not think they can be kept together, as the boys are much the sharpest. This made a class of 15. I went on with "practice" as before.
[West, Ann
Butcher, Emma
Simms, Sarah
Reeves, Clara
Daw, Emma
Dawson, Lydia
Park, Eliza.]
Began a MS book for miscellaneous entries of anything worth remembering and referring to, which belongs to no special book. ["Miscellanea."][63]

---

63. The book titled "Miscellanea" has not survived. See n. *51* above.

> Gordon suggested a question in Ancient mathematics: *viz.* how did the Romans work multiplication? He, Lloyd, and I, tried it, but could not make much of it.[64]

Feb: 2. (Sat).   Called on the Dean, (my third call this term), to consult him on subjects connected with the Mathematical Lecture. [Mrs. C. Kean was a Miss Ellen Tree.]

Frank arrived unexpectedly in the evening: he does not yet know the result of his Woolwich examination: (*Page* was one of the candidates.)[65]

Ordered at Slatters' the rest of the *Gilfillan's Poets*: all for 1854 and 1855 (except Dryden) were sent over.[66]

---

64.   Multiplication in Roman numerals is particularly difficult since the number system is not based on the principles of place-value, the basis of the decimal system of Arabic numerals in general use today. Instead it uses a series of letters to represent various numerical values. The construction of Roman numerals and their computational procedures, such as multiplication and subtraction, follow relatively complex algorithms which make them impracticable and hence they have only historic interest today. Osborne Gordon (1813-83); see *Diary 1*, p. 58 n.*26*.

65.   See n. *32* above. One of the other candidates known to Dodgson was probably Herbert William Cobbold Page who matriculated at Christ Church in June 1854 from Eton, aged 18. He eventually took his B.A. at New Inn Hall in 1859.

66.   Issued as separate critiques for each poet, but normally found as *The Poetical Works of Goldsmith, Collins, and T. Warton. With lives, critical dissertations, and explanatory notes by the Rev. G{eorge}*

Feb: 5. (Tu). Varied the lesson at the school with a story, introducing a number of sums to be worked out. I also worked for them the puzzle of writing the answer to an addition sum, when only one of the five rows have been written: this, and the trick of counting alternately up to 100, neither putting on more than 10 to the number last named, astonished them not a little.[67]

Sent a copy of "The Palace of Humbug" to *Punch*, as a last experiment in favour of that unfortunate poem, which has already been sent to the *Comic Times* and *Train* without effect.[68]

I am resolved once more to make an attempt at something like a system of

---

Gilfillan (Edinburgh: 1854) and *The Poetical Works of Johnson, Parnell, Gray and Smollett. With memoirs, critical dissertations, and explanatory notes by the Rev. G. Gilfillan* (Edinburgh: 1855). Dodgson had 48 volumes of Gilfillan's *The British Poets with Memoirs and Critical Dissertations* in his library (see *Library* p. 42 lot 854 and p. 51 lot 977).

67. These mathematical tricks became part of his repertoire for entertaining children and probably would have been included in his projected book of games and puzzles which was in preparation at the time of his death. The "starting with the answer" problem involves the complements of 9 which are added to give pairs of results which are one less than a power of 10. By working in this way, it is a straightforward matter to predict the eventual answer. See *Games and Puzzles*, volume 2, for a detailed explanation of this puzzle. The other number trick is difficult to identify from this brief explanation, but a similar technique was used in Dodgson's game "Arithmetical Croquet."

68. "The Palace of Humbug," see n. *20* above.

reading. I shall not try for regular quantities or hours: it must fit in as well as it can with the paramount work of the lecture. The plan I have resolved on is:

First, *Monday and Thursday*: *Greek*. Beginning with *Thucydides*, right through.

Second, *Tuesday and Friday*: *Latin*. Beginning with *Horace*, right through. In both of these books I shall take the rule "at the end of a chapter review the chapter: at the end of a book review the book" etc.

Third, *History*, at present English. I shall no longer try to master whole periods, a feat I have long despaired of. I believe the best way is to take one single point (I shall begin with the Reformation), and get it up thoroughly, and so on. Thoroughness must be the rule of all this reading.[69]

---

69.   Dodgson's reading plan is supported by his development of a comprehensive personal library which eventually housed more than 4,000 books. For his Greek reading he selects *Thucydides*. He owned a copy of Arnold's *Thucydides* (see *Library*, p. 18 lot 382) and a collected edition of *Thucydides Works* annotated in his hand (see *Library*, p. 86 lot 338). His Latin reading consisted of Horace (see *Library*, p. 24 lots 477 & 478; p. 25 lot 507; p. 41 lot 837; and p. 54 lot 1086). He also owned a number of history texts but found this a difficult subject to accomplish with any level of personal satisfaction. See n. *114* below. The source of Dodgson's quoted rule for reviewing chapters and books has not been identified.

Feb: 6. (W).   Sent a copy of my verses on "Solitude" to Mr. Yates for the *Train*.[70]
[inserted in No.3 March 1856]
Got Haydn's *Dictionary of Dates*.[71]

Feb: 7. (Th).   A woman of St. Ebbe's parish called to ask for charity, her husband, Stephen Lake, being laid up and out of work. I promised to speak to Mr. Cameron about her.[72]
Dined at the Senior Master's table, as I was the only junior in Hall.

Feb: 8. (F).   The school class noisy and inattentive, the novelty of the thing is wearing off, and I find them rather unmanageable. Showed them the "9" trick of striking out a figure, after subtracting a number from its

---

70.   "Solitude," see n. *104* below.

71.   Joseph Haydn's *Dictionary of Dates, and universal reference, relating to all ages and nations ... With copious details of England, Scotland, and Ireland* (London: 1841). Dodgson probably acquired the seventh edition dated 1855 "... *with additions and corrections by B. Vincent.*"

72.   George Thomas Cameron, M.A., curate of St. Ebbe's. The reason that Mr. Stephen Lake lost his position at work is not identified. See also 9 February, below. Dodgson made a discretionary payment to the Lakes on 13 February using Cameron as his intermediary. The matter then appears to have been closed.

reverse.[73] Was a good deal tired with the six hours' consecutive lecturing.

Heard from Mr. Yates. He is going to use the verses on "Solitude," and the "Carpette Knyghte," he wishes me to alter the signature B.B. and proposed that I should adopt some *nom de plume*: accordingly I sent "Dares," at the same time I suggested a picture to illustrate the verses, if Bennett will deign to draw it, a group of children at play.[74]

Read third number of *Little Dorrit*.[75]

Feb: 9. (Sat). Wrote to Swabey, asking him to make out for me whether the case of Stephen Lake is a proper one for charity. At the same time I asked what he considered the best way for my going on at the school: my own idea is to form a new class,

---

73. The nine-trick puzzle concerns a mathematical outcome when a number is subtracted from its reverse; the sum of the digits in the result is always divisible by 9. By "striking out" one of the digits in the answer, it is possible to determine this number from the sum of the remaining digits. For example, subtracting 3725 from its reverse 5273 gives an answer of 1548. By striking out the numeral 4 and finding the sum of the remaining digits gives 14. Subtract this from the next highest multiple of 9, namely 18, gives 4, the missing digit.

74. Dodgson's pseudonym did not meet Yates' approval. See 10, 11 February, below. Charles Henry Bennett (1829-67); see *Diary 1*, p. 117 n.*142*.

75. Dickens' *Little Dorrit* appeared as a series of separately published instalments between 1855 and 1857.

consisting only of the bright and attentive boys and girls: the system of taking the whole of the two first classes does not answer well.

Question: when we are dreaming and, as often happens, have a dim consciousness of the fact and try to wake, do we not say and do things which in waking life would be insane? May we not then sometimes define insanity as an inability to distinguish which is the waking and which the sleeping life? We often dream without the least suspicion of unreality: "sleep hath its own world," and it is often as lifelike as the other.[76]

Feb: 10.(Sun). Heard again from Mr. Yates, he wants me to choose another name, as Dares is too much like a newspaper signature. [With reference to the picture[77] (see Feb: 8.) he says he has already handed the verses over for illustration, and that the idea he gave the artist was, a man lying stretched under a large tree on a hill, a brook meandering in the distance, and a general

---

76.   Dodgson's view of the dream-state, an idea he eventually used to great effect in both *Alice* books, became a fundamental feature of *Sylvie & Bruno* and *Sylvie and Bruno Concluded*.

77.   The illustration for "Solitude" drawn by Charles Bennett appeared in *The Train*, much as described here.

sense of solitude and stillness pervading the picture.] Dined with Fowler at Lincoln, met Pattison, Tristram, and a Mr. Walesby, the other coach in law.[78]

Feb: 11. (M).   Wrote to Mr. Yates, sending him a choice of names, 1. *Edgar Cuthwellis* (made by transposition out of "Charles Lutwidge"), 2. *Edgar U. C. Westhill* (ditto), 3. *Louis Carroll* (derived from Lutwidge = Ludovic = Louis, and Charles), 4. *Lewis Carroll* (ditto).
[Mar: 1. *Lewis Carroll* was chosen.][79]

---

78.   Mark Pattison (1813-84), matriculated at Oriel College in 1832 and gained his B.A. in 1836. He became Fellow of Lincoln College between 1839-60. He was Greek lecturer in 1841, tutor from 1842-55, bursar in 1843 and sub-rector in 1846. He eventually became delegate of the University Press and Curator of the Bodleian Library. He was made Rector of Lincoln College in 1861 until his death. He was author of many books including *The Life of Casaubon*. Thomas Hutchinson Tristram matriculated at Lincoln College on 11 November 1843, aged 18, and was an exhibitioner from 1843-51. He took his B.C.L. in 1850 and his D.C.L. in 1854. He was an advocate to the Doctors' Commons in 1855. He became a Q.C. in 1881 and later judge of the Consistory Court of London. He was also made chancellor of the Diocese of Hereford and of Ripon, and commissary-general of the Diocese of Canterbury later in his career. Francis Pearson Walesby (1798-1858) matriculated at Wadham College in 1816. He was a Fellow of Lincoln from 1824-37, holding the post of bursar in 1828. He became a barrister-at-law at Gray's Inn in 1826. He was Rawlinsonian Professor of Anglo-Saxon from 1829-34.

79.   Dodgson did not use the pseudonym, Lewis Carroll, exclusively from this time. For example, in *College Rhymes* (1860-3), he made a number of contribution using the pen-names, Lewis Carroll, B.B. and R.W.G. The latter is probably from his real name taking the fourth letter in each of Charles Lutwidge Dodgson. Eventually, Lewis Carroll became the preferred pen-name.

1856

Feb: 12. (Tu). Heard from Menella Smedley, with corrections for the sonnet I wrote for Mary's book etc. She also asks me to make out under what regulations the *Oxford and Cambridge Magazine* is published, and if feminine contributions could possibly gain insertion.[80]

Swabey met me at the school to settle about the class, and I agreed to try a little longer taking the whole of both classes, and set them sums all round, so as to give each something to do. I taught them a little about fractions, and explained the trick of the addition sum. Swabey also brought me a note from Cameron, saying that the Lakes are just now really in distress, but that the woman is a confirmed beggar.

Gordon showed us in the Common Room a toad he has had given him, which was found buried in a mass of hardened clay, under a layer of coal: it is alive, and seems likely to live.

---

80.   The sonnet in Mary's book underwent a number of corrections and changes, but sadly does not seem to have survived (see n. *15* above). *The Oxford and Cambridge Magazine* appeared throughout 1856, financed, in the main edited, and in part written, by William Morris. The other contributors were from his "set," notably Edward Burne Jones, R. W. Dixon and Cormell Price . Rossetti contributed to the later numbers, and there were a few articles by Cambridge men. The only female contributor was Georgiana MacDonald, soon to become Mrs. Burne Jones. Dodgson does not appear to have known any of this interesting "set" mainly drawn from Exeter and Pembroke Colleges, but not long afterwards met Rossetti.

[Epigram (on a toad) by my father.

Rusticus, ut massam cretæ diffindit aratro,
Bufonem e medio prosiluisse videt.
Unde ortus? pastus? plane est Cretensis et αργην γαστερα,
Cretenses qua celebrantur, habet.

Added by Gordon.

Quæritur unde ortus: sed nil quæramus ab ipso:
Κρητεν αυ ψενσταυ credite Κρησι nihil.][81]

Feb: 13. (W). Sent Cameron five shillings for the benefit of the Lakes, saying at the same time that I meant to refuse the woman assistance in future, (as he gives her the character of a regular beggar) unless she could bring a special note of recommendation from him.

My reading scheme is failing: it is in fact nearly impossible to do more in the day than the work of the lecture.

---

81.   The Latin and Greek translates: "A peasant, as he is breaking up a lump of chalky soil with the plough, sees a toad which has sprung out of the middle of it. Where did it come from? How was it nourished? It is obviously Cretan and has an idle belly, a characteristic for which Cretans are famed." Gordon's addition says: "The question is asked, where did it come from: but let us ask nothing of the toad itself: whether he is made of chalk or is a cheat, give no credence to Cretans." There is a verbal play on the word "cretæ" (chalk) and "cres/cretis" (an inhabitant of Crete). The phrase "idle belly" means someone who does not work for his living.

1856

Called on Scoltock, who has been ill. Walked with Bradshaw.[82]

Feb: 15. (F).   School class again noisy and troublesome. I have not yet acquired the art of keeping order.

I am thinking of writing an article on "Cipher" for the *Train*, but must first consult Mr. Yates as to whether the subject will be admissible.[83]

Feb: 18. (M).   Walked with Scoltock in the afternoon.

Feb: 19. (Tu).   School class better, as I threatened to banish those who did not attend from the lesson.

I found an old book the other day in the Library, with a head of Janus done in pen and ink, and the motto, (probably the old one of the family) *Respice et*

---

82.   William Scoltock (1823-86), Christ Church graduate, took his M.A. in 1846, who went on to become an inspector of schools. On his death, he left some important paintings by Gainsborough, Cuyp and Hals initially to his niece, Miss S. A. Parker, but eventually to the Dean and Chapter of Christ Church, to be placed in the Common Room (see *Oxford Pamphlets*, p. 276). Robert William Bradshaw matriculated in 1855 aged 18 and eventually gained his B.A. in 1859 and went on to become a student at Lincoln's Inn.

83.   Dodgson devised a number of ciphers including a matrix cipher (see 23 February 1858), the telegraph cipher (see 22 April 1868) and the alphabet cipher (not mentioned in his diary, but closely linked to the telegraph cipher).

Resipisce. There was also *In futurum et provectum,* which most likely was added as an explanation, and did not belong to the original motto.[84]

Feb: 21. (Th).   Spent the hour in the Library looking over indexes of histories of shires etc. in search of the name Dodgson. I found the two given opposite: there are many instances of it in a history of Leeds, which I will add.[85]
[1517. John Dodgson, Mayor of York.
1540. William Dodgson (merchant) ditto]

Feb: 25. (M).   First afternoon of the torpids. Frank and I went down to see them and fell in with the Liddell party. (Mrs. L., her sister, and the two eldest children). We bumped University, and are now second.[86]

---

84.   The Dodgson family motto translates: "Look back and see reason." The addition says: "Carried also into the future."

85.   The Dodgson ancestry, fully researched and traced by Roger Lancelyn Green, is identified and explained in his introduction reprinted in *Diary 1.*

86.   This is the first recorded meeting of Dodgson with members of Dean Liddell's family. The party consisted of Mrs Lorina Hannah Liddell (1826-1910) née Reeve, her sister Pleasance Elizabeth Fellowes (married Rev. Thomas John Lyon Fellowes), and the two eldest Liddell children, Edward Henry "Harry" (1847-1911) and Lorina Charlotte (1849-1930). Torpids are University boat races. College boats leave the starting point in order of success in previous races; bumping a boat means that the crew gains position over the boat which has been caught..

1856

[I find Mayo is an old friend of Mr. Yates. They were at school together at Highgate. Ranken was also one of his schoolfellows.][87]

Feb: 26. (Tu). Class again noisy and inattentive, it is very disheartening, and I almost think I had better give up teaching there for the present.

    Went to the first of Jacobson's lectures.[88]

    Borrowed Bon Gaultier's *Ballads of Crewe*, they are very clever, but spoil the beautiful originals.[89]

Feb: 29. (F). Left word at the school that I shall not be able to come again for the present. I doubt if I shall try again next term: the good done does not seem worth the time and trouble.

    I have been trying for the last two days to solve a problem in chances, given

---

87.   William Henry Ranken (1832-1904); see *Diary 1*, p. 59 n. *28*.

88.   William Jacobson (1803-84), Canon of Christ Church and Regius Professor of Divinity, later Bishop of Chester.

89.   Bon Gaultier, pseudonym of Sir Theodore Martin, and William Edmonstoune Aytoun, published a volume of parodies, *The Book of Ballads* in 1845. A *New Edition, with several new ballads. Illustrated by A. Crowquill, R. Doyle and J. Leech* was published in London in 1849. Dodgson later acquired a copy of Bon Gaultier's *Ballads*, an illustrated edition dated 1859 (see *Library*, p. 42 lot 848).

me by Pember, which is said to have raised much discussion in the college. It is an exceedingly complicated question, and I have not yet got near a solution.[90]
[Problem in the game of "Sympathy."
The game is this: two players lay out two separate packs in heaps of 3, (and one card over in each pack), turning each top card face upwards, so as to have 18 faces on each side. Those which correspond are paired off together, and the cards under them turned face up: (the simplest way would be, to lay all face up originally).

Required: the chance of the whole pack being paired off in this way.]

Mar: 1. (Sat). Received an invitation to a musical party at the Deanery next Saturday.

Somerset was seized with a fit this morning in the passage leading from the Anatomical School Quadrangle. I was passing through at the moment, and caught him as he fell: having no idea what the nature of the fit was, I could think of nothing but loosening everything

---

90.　Edward Henry Pember (1833-?) was a Student at Christ Church 1854-61, took his B.A. in 1854 with a first in classics and a third in law and history. He became a barrister at Lincoln's Inn in 1858, Q. C. in 1874 and a bencher in 1876. There is no indication whether Dodgson eventually solved Pember's probability problem. The topic certainly interested him and he went on to include probability problems of his own devising in *Curiosa Mathematica Part II, Pillow Problems* (1893).

about the neck, and dashing some water in his face. Luckily there was a doctor in the Anatomy School, who was brought by one of the men bringing coals who happened to be there. He pronounced it to be epilepsy, and said he had better lie still some time and then be got to his rooms: he and Southey and I half led, half carried him to his rooms by the meadow gate, and there the Doctor (a Dr. Dowson, whom I remember to have met at Whitby) had to leave him. Dr. Hitchings soon after arrived, and made him go to bed for the rest of the day. I sat there for some time, then Southey relieved guard, and Joyce afterwards took the post for the afternoon, by which time a nurse had been procured. I am thankful that I was passing at the moment, and so had an opportunity of being of use in an emergency. I felt at the moment how helpless ignorance makes one, and I shall make a point of reading some book on the subject of emergencies, a thing that I think every one should do.[91]

---

91.   Raglan George Henry Somerset (1831-?), third son of Lord Granville Somerset, matriculated at Christ Church in 1849; B.A. 1853; M.A. 1856; Student from 1849-67, and a gentleman usher to Queen Victoria. His fit was attended by Dr. John Dowson (M.D. Glasgow; M.R.C.S. England) and also Dr. G. C. H. Hitchings, medical practitioner of Holywell Street. This event may have been the catalyst for Dodgson's lifelong interest in medical matters. See also n. *93* below.

In the evening I went to one of Mitford's Harmonic parties, and heard some fair ordinary songs, and capital comic singing and acting by Twiss, *Macbeth*, *The Country Fair*, and *Richard III*.[92]

Mar: 4. (Tu). Ordered *Hints for Emergencies*.[93]

Mar: 5. (W). Went to the theatre to hear Monk's musical exercise for the degree of Doctor of Music, *Gray's Bard*.[94] The place was densely crowded: some of the music very fine. I liked best the Aria "Girt with many a barm bold." The solos were sung by a Mr. Thomas.

Dined with Fowler at Lincoln, to meet Ranken, he proposes that we should go to Whitby or somewhere together this next Vacation.

---

92. Quintin William Francis Twiss (1835-?), a Student at Christ Church who took his B.A. in 1857 and his M.A. in 1860. Although renowned as an amateur actor, he became a clerk in the treasury in 1856.

93. No medical book with this title appears in Dodgson's library although there are several on a similar topic, such as *Household Medicine and Sick Room Guide* and *The Traveller's Medical Companion*. See *Library*, p. 27 lot 536, and p. 80 lot 127.

94. Edwin George Monk, matriculated at Exeter College on 1 December 1848, aged 28, and gained his B. Mus. relatively quickly indicating a musician of talent. He gained his D. Mus. on 15 March 1856, a few days after Dodgson heard him play his doctorate exercises.

Mar: 6. (Th).   Finished lectures for the term, and took a holiday. Made friends with little Harry Liddell, (whom I first spoke to down at the boats last week): he is certainly the handsomest boy I ever saw.[95] Gave Price the problem in "Sympathy," (see Feb: 29) the solution being beyond my powers, (except with the help of logarithms).

Mar: 8. (Sat).   Went to the Deanery in the evening to a musical party: about half the college were there. The songs in *Macbeth* were the chief performance: a son of Chevalier Bunsen sung some things magnificently: among others, *Blücher's War Song.*[96] The choruses were taken by Pember and his brother, Mitford, Twiss etc. The party broke up about half past eleven. I took the opportunity of making friends with little

---

95.   Edward Henry "Harry" Liddell (1847-1911) was the first member of the Dean's family to be befriended by Dodgson. Offers to teach him mathematics prior to his entering school proved less successful than instruction in rowing on the river. Harry Liddell later married Mary Cory in 1876. After his first wife's death in 1905, he married Ethel Sophia Gresham in 1907.

96.   The son of Chevalier Bunsen was Ernest de Bunsen (1819-1903) who, after serving in the Prussian army and at the Prussian legation, settled in London and was known for his literary and Biblical studies and his musical abilities. His father was Baron Bunsen, the German diplomatist, who married the Welsh heiress, Frances Waddington. *Blücher's War Song* was sung by German soldiers in the Army of the Rhine. An English translation was made by A. B. Farnie (1870) and Speranza (1874).

Lorina Liddell, the second of the family.[97]

Mar: 9. (Sun). Frank got his commission.

Mar: 10. (M). Wrote a fragment of burlesque on ancient Tragedy. I mean to work it up to a complete play, and send it to William Wilcox for his "Whitburniana." [98] I think also of completing a poem (begun long ago) for the *Train*, and calling it "The Path of Roses." I have been adding to it lately with this idea.[99] Sent the numbers of the *Train* by Blackmore to Arnold, to ask if he would contribute anything. Blackmore tells me that he has written a good deal in magazines. [He consented, and means to send an essay on *Hypatia*.][100]

---

97. Although Dodgson met seven year old Lorina Liddell on 25 February, this was his first opportunity to get more acquainted with her.

98. "Whitburniana" was probably a family magazine written by his cousin, William Edward Wilcox (1835-1918). No copy is known. Likewise, Dodgson's fragment of ancient tragedy has not survived. The Wilcox family lived at Whitburn, hence the title. See *Diary 1*, p. 124 n. *154*.

99. "The Path of Roses" appeared in *The Train*. See n. *104* below.

100. Richard Blackmore matriculated at Christ Church on 18 October 1854, aged 19, and gained his B.A. in 1858. He took his M.A. in 1861 and became vicar of Merther, Cornwall, in 1868. Frederick Arnold (1833-91) matriculated at Christ Church on 24 January 1856, aged 23, and gained his B.A. in 1860. He was the author of various works and sometime editor of the *Literary Gazette*.

1856

Decided on going round by London to hear Jenny Lind in the *Messiah* on Tuesday, and wrote to Uncle Hassard, to ask him to get me a ticket.[101] Frank is to find me a bed somewhere in Putney: I am ashamed of quartering myself again in Brompton so soon.

Mar: 11. (Tu). Had Fowler to dinner.

[Mar: 12. (W). Discovered a principle (probably long known), of making a winning book on any race where *the sum of the chances* (according to market odds) *is not exactly one.* Reduce to a common denominator: put that back into odds, and make your bets in sums proportional to those numbers, *giving all* the odds if the sum of the chances *exceeds* one, and *vice versa*]

Mar: 14. (F). Left Oxford by the 4.40 and arrived in Putney about half past eight.

Easter Vacation

Mar: 14. (F). Arrived in Putney about 8.30, only Uncle Hassard, Frank, Lucy, Percy, Charlotte, and Jimmy are here: the rest are at

---

101. Dodgson heard Jenny Lind (1821-85) sing in Handel's *Messiah* at Exeter Hall on 18 March.

Richmond (some at Ham), to get rid of the hooping cough by change of air.

Mar: 15. (Sat). Went over with the party to Richmond, and left Charlotte there. They all look well but Marla, who seems a good deal pulled down, and is beginning, I am afraid, to have the peculiar stunted look of Charlotte and Amy.[102] Uncle Skeffington leaves Brompton today for a professional tour, so that I miss seeing him.[103]

[Oxford and Cambridge boat race. Frank and I were in one of the attendant steamers. We lost by about half a length, after a most evenly contested race, said to be the best ever seen here. It is said that we should have won, if we had taken the same line as Cambridge, so as to have the tide with us all the way: by bad steering we seem to have got occasionally into back-water.]

Mar: 16.(Sun). After morning service, Frank and I went into London, to call on Mr. Yates, whom we found at home. He seemed glad to

---

102.   Marla is Dodgson's cousin, Menella Frances, then aged eight, sister of Charlotte and Amy.

103.   Skeffington Lutwidge was a Commissioner in Lunacy, and this was probably the reason for his professional tour.

1856

hear of Arnold's intended paper. I
mentioned various subjects I thought of
writing on: (1) Nursery Songs, (2)
Cipher, (3) Paradoxes, (4) Betting, all but
the last he seemed to approve of: the first
highly. He acknowledges the error of
having two stories going on at once, and
says that "Mr. Watkin's Apprentice" is to
wind up in another number or two. Albert
Smith, who is an intimate friend of his,
has offered to write him an article on
Evan's Hotel, but dare not give his name,
as he has already refused to write for
Fraser and *Blackwood*.[104] I was very glad
to hear from him that he has a great
quantity of copy in hand, and if he can
only keep on until *Little Dorrit* is over, he
hopes to make a position: at present,
Dickens may be depriving him of many
possible readers, as so many people will

---

104.   Edmund Hodgson Yates (1831-94) became editor of *The Train* in 1856
following the demise of *The Comic Times*. Dodgson contributed eight
items to the five half-yearly volumes eventually produced, but these did
not include the proposed subjects listed here. His contributions were
"Solitude," "Yᵉ Carpette Knyghte," "The Path of Roses," "The Three
Voices," "Upon the Lonely Moor," "Novelty and Romancement," "The
Sailor's Wife" and "Hiawatha's Photographing" which is not mentioned in
this volume of the Diaries. See also *Diary 1*, p. 112 n. *131*. "Mr. Watkins's
Apprentice" was a serialised story by William Brough (1826-70), begun in
the first issue and continued throughout the first volume for eight
chapters. The other concurrent story was "Marston Lynch" by Robert
Barnabas Brough (1828-60) which ran for 31 chapters throughout the first
four volumes. Albert Smith (1816-60) did not produce the article about
Evan's Hotel.

only take in one monthly periodical. We went to see the remains of Covent Garden Theatre on our way back, but could not get near to it anywhere, as the police have put up barricades in all the approaches: the whole front, and indeed the whole outer shell, seems to be still entire. *The Times* account led one to think that nothing was left standing.[105]

Mar: 17. (M). Called on Southey in the morning, and agreed to go together tomorrow and buy a photographic apparatus.

Mar: 18. (Tu). Went again to Southey, and reached Harley Street about 1. We went to a maker of the name of Ottewill, in Charlotte Street, Caledonian Road: the camera with lens etc. will come to just

---

105. The fire at Covent Garden Theatre occurred on 5 March during the early hours of the morning. The theatre was leased to John Anderson for a ten week season. On the final night of his tenancy, 4 March, he arranged a "Bal Masque" which lasted throughout the night. At five o'clock in the morning, as the National Anthem was being played, the fire warning was given. Fire engines from all over London attended but could not save the building. The roof collapsed and the theatre was destroyed [*Covent Garden* by Mary Cathcart Bover: 1967]. *The Times* reported on 5 March, "Total Destruction of Covent Garden Theatre: The most magnificent lyric temple in Europe was this morning reduced to a mass of shapeless ruins by a fire which broke out from some hitherto unexplained cause in the roof of the theatre, immediately over the stage.... Of the theatre not a vestige is saved: nothing but the bare walls is left standing..." A more detailed account of the fire appeared in the following day's issue of *The Times* and on 7 March, the paper reported immense numbers of people visiting the scene of the fire.

about £15. I ordered it to be sent to Ch. Ch. as it will not be ready in time to do anything this vacation.

Exeter Hall in the evening, to hear the *Messiah*; singers, Jenny Lind, Miss Dolby, Mr. Lockey, Mr. Weiss, and Mr. Swift.[106] Jenny Lind was much older looking than I expected to see: her settled expression seems sincere, but this changed as she sang into a beautiful sweet smile, and she seemed to abandon herself to the glorious music with almost a child's delight. Nothing that I can conceive in singing could be more delicious than her high notes, so sweet and low as to {be} more like singing in a dream. Miss Dolby sang, to my ear, to perfection, and I do not think I ever enjoyed anything more than her "He shall feed his flock like a shepherd." Two other of my favourites were "I know that my Redeemer liveth" by Jenny Lind, and "Why do the nations so furiously rage together" by Mr. Weiss.

This day I mark with a white stone.

Mar: 19. (W). Went over to Richmond for the afternoon,

---

106.   Charlotte Helen Sainton-Dolby (1821-85) contralto for whom Mendelssohn wrote his *Elijah*. Willoughby Hunter Weiss (1820-67) vocalist and composer who wrote the music to Longfellow's "Village Blacksmith."

and walked in the park with the party. Wrote to ask Mr. Yates what is the last day in the month for sending in contributions.
[He says the 15th.]

Mar: 20. (Th). Came down to Ripon by the Great Northern, and fell in with Charles Tate at York.[107] He is with an architect there. Lodged with Burnett, the Dean's verger.[108]

Mar: 22. (Sat). To the Palace in the morning, with Elizabeth and my father: the Longleys, all but Caroline and Rosamond, are going to London for some weeks.
[Henry
George
Mary Henrietta
Fanny
Arthur
Caroline Georgina
Rosamond Esther Harriet][109]

---

107.   Charles Grey Tate (1836-1900), son of James Tate (see *Diary 1*, p. 115).

108.   William Burnett (c. 1788-1858), third child of Robert Burnett, a farmer of Fawdington in the parish of Cundall, Yorks., and his wife Hannah. He married Jane Chambers in 1828 at Ripon Cathedral, where he was the Dean's verger, a position he held until his death.

109.   Dodgson's monograms for Caroline and Rosamond were added. See n. *4* & n. *10* above. Also Arthur Longley (1841-1920).

Mar: 24. (M). Got *House out of Windows* and *Away with Melancholy* from London,[110] and read aloud the latter in the afternoon to the party, including Miss Erskine, and Caroline and Rosamond Longley with Miss Lee the governess: they had been spending the day with the children dyeing Easter eggs.[111]

Mar: 25. (Tu). Went over to the Palace with Aunt Lucy Lutwidge to take Henrietta and Edwin to spend the afternoon with the Longleys.

Mar: 26. (W). Went with the party to see the Crimean photographs, now exhibiting in Ripon, and met the Longleys there.[112] Party at the

---

110.   *House out of Windows* was a one-act farce by William Brough (1826-70), writer for *The Train*. *Away with Melancholy* , another farce in one act by John Maddison Morton was one of Dodgson's favourite plays; see *Diary 1*, pp. 105 n. *118*, 128, 132. The play was adapted from a French dramatisation by Delacour, de la Rounat and Montjoye, entitled *Un Homme entre deux Airs*. The play was published in a series called *Lacy's Acting Editions* (1850), and it was a copy of this book which Dodgson purchased and read as part of evening entertainments.

111.   For details of Miss Erskine, see n. *9* above. Emma Lee (1823-?) was governess to the children of Charles Thomas Longley, Bishop of Ripon. She was the daughter of Robert and Ann Lee from Stoke Newington. Her father was an assistant teacher at Bransby's Academy.

112.   This is probably the famous series of 350 Crimean War pictures taken between March and June 1855 by Roger Fenton (1819-69), founder and first secretary of the Photographic Society of London, later the Royal Photographic Society of Great Britain, which was first exhibited in London during the previous October.

Residence, including the Battyes, a Mr. Wood etc. Mr. Wood is a lawyer:[113] he tells me that the author of *Law versus Love, or the Deceased Wife's Sister*, is a friend of his, Joseph Middleton.[114]

Mar: 27. (Th). Finished *Heartsease*:[115] the characters of Theodora and Percy are well conceived, and Violet is also clever, but the story generally wants form and incident. The fire and falling in of the coal-pit are about as much connected with the story as the

---

113.   William Walker Battye (1797-?), son of Richard Battye of Crosland Manor, near Huddersfield, and his wife Mary Walker; married Margaret Scholefield in 1827; was a magistrate living at Ingerthorpe Grange, near Ripon. The family later moved to Skelton Hall, near York. Their only son was Richard Battye (1834-73), a barrister and J.P. Thomas Wood (c. 1821-96), second son of John Wood of Harewood Lodge and his wife Martha, daughter of Richard Hirst of Meltham, Yorks.; B.A. Trinity College, Cambridge 1845; admitted at the Inner Temple 1843; called to the Bar 1848; married Caroline Martha, only daughter of John Harrison, banker of Bellwood, Ripon, in 1845. The Woods lived at West Grange, Ripon, and later moved to Bellwood. Their only son was Arthur John Harrison Wood, born 1847, married Rosamund Swire in 1872.

114.   Joseph Middleton, barrister-at-law, wrote *Law; or Marriage with a Deceased Wife's Sister* in 1855.

115.   *Heartsease; or, the Brother's Wife* by Charlotte Mary Yonge (1823-1901), published in 1854. Arthur Martindale, a thoughtless and selfish Guards' officer marries the beautiful sixteen-year-old Violet, but keeps the wedding a secret from his aristocratic parents, until finally his child-bride is launched on the formidable family without support and guidance. Theodora was Arthur's sister, and Percy his brother. Charlotte Yonge edited *The Monthly Packet* from 1851 to 1894 to which Dodgson contributed the whole of *A Tangled Tale* as a series of "Knots" (1880-85) and other puzzles and games including three versions of *Lanrick*.

accidents in a newspaper are with the leaders.

Mar: 29. (Sat). Expedition to Macleshaw {sic} and Studley. Frances Jane, Elizabeth Lucy, and downwards; Miss {Harriet} and Miss Agnes Erskine, and Caroline and Rosamond Longley with Miss Lee. The day was beautiful and most enjoyable.[116]

Mar: 31. (M). Went over to Stainley with Elizabeth Lucy, Caroline Hume and Mary Charlotte to take Edwin back to school.[117] Afterwards with the rest of the party to the Palace to bid goodbye.

News of the signing of Peace came by telegraph. The cathedral bells were ringing most of the day, and flags flying all over the town. Thus March does for

---

116. Mackershaw (not Macleshaw), a wooded area alongside the River Skell in Studley Park, not far from Ripon. The party included Dodgson's sisters Frances and Elizabeth and other members of the family (hence his reference "downwards") together with the group he was with on 24 March. Also Agnes Erskine (1825-1912), daughter of the Dean of Ripon.

117. Edwin's preparatory school, before going to Twyford, was run by the incumbent of North Stainley, Joseph Jefferson (1818-82), curate from 1851-81. Just prior to Jefferson's move to North Stainley, he lived with his parents at Sharow, near Ripon, and ran a school with the help of his sister, Eliza; his pupils included Albert Charles Wood of Hollin Hall (see n. *15* above). Jefferson expanded his school-mastering business at North Stainley Parsonage with his sister as teacher, and a further schoolmaster, Samuel Hairsine, and his wife, both assisting with the teaching. In 1861, the school had 12 boy pupils, all under the age of 14 years.

once "go out like a lamb," leaving us once more in peace, *quo sit perpetua!*[118]

Ap: 1. (Tu).   The party returned to Croft.

Ap: 3. (Th).   Heard the singing lesson in the school, about 50 are learning, and there are many good voices among them: one piece they sang in full harmony. They are also learning a choral service, which Mr. Baker hopes to introduce in church on week days.[119]

Ap: 4. (F).   Called, with Elizabeth Lucy and Caroline Hume, on Mr. Brown of Darlington, who has just been presented to a new living, Redmarshall, a few miles further north.[120]

---

118.   Peace in the Crimean War was signed on 30 March without advantage to either Russia or Britain and her allies. During the campaign, Britain lost 19,600 soldiers, mainly from disease and privation. The Latin translates: "may it last!"

119.   James Baker (1823-?), first son of Rev. James Baker; University College, Oxford, B.A. 1847; M.A. 1851; ordained deacon 1852; priest 1853; curate Gt. Milton, Oxon. 1852-4; curate Croft, Yorks. 1855-8; chaplain Winchester College 1858; rector St. Swithin, Winchester 1859-63; chaplain Hampshire County Hospital 1885.

120.   George Brown (c.1800-88), educated at Durham University 1838; ordained priest Durham 1838; perpetual curate Darlington St. John 1844-56; rector Redmarshall, Stockton, 1856 until his death. He married Ann Webster in 1839 and they had at least 14 children. He was the author of *The Volume of Creation*, *Gleanings in Natural Theology* and *A Manual of Divinity*.

1856

Ap: 5. (Sat).   Left Croft for Oxford.

Easter and Act Term 1856

Ap: 5. (Sat).   Arrived in Ch. Ch. about 10 at night, and found Frank arrived: he is going to reside this term, as he has arranged to wait for the next batch of novices at Woolwich.

Ap: 8. (Tu).   A letter appeared in *The Times*, from "Jellinger Symons," denying the rotation of the moon.[121] I sent an answer, a sort of practical illustration of the necessity of its rotation. In considering the subject, I noticed for the first time the fact that though it only goes 13 times round the

---

121.   A letter under the title "The Moon Has No Rotary Motion" appeared in *The Times* on 8 April signed by Jelinger Symons, Her Majesty's Inspector of Schools. The letter begins: "May I request the favour of a small space in your columns to inquire the grounds upon which almost all school astronomy books assert that the moon rotates on her axis?" He goes on to say that since only one side of the moon's surface is ever visible from the earth, it does in fact not rotate on its axis. The following day *The Times* reported a vast postbag of replies and printed seven letters as a representative sample of the responses. Dodgson's reply did not appear. Jelinger Symons wrote again on 14 April still denying the rotation of the moon and Dodgson penned another reply. On 15 April, a letter was printed concentrating on the geometrical principles involved in the problem, but since it was signed by E.B.D. this is unlikely to be by Dodgson even accounting for a transcription error with his initials. The controversy rolled on throughout the month with further letters from Symons and other correspondents. Dodgson does not appear to have written any further letters, probably sensing that with two replies already rejected there is little chance of getting another contribution accepted. See also 14 April, below.

earth in the course of the year, it makes 14 revolutions round its own axis, the extra one being due to its motion round the sun.

Bought *My Haunts* by E. H. Yates.[122]

Ap: 10. (Th). Copied in the Library part of an old map of Yorkshire (containing Croft).

Finished and sent "The Path of Roses" to Mr. Yates for the *Train*. At the same time I suggested a subject for an illustration, basing it on the concluding lines of the poem. The lady standing near the window where the sun's last rays are streaming in: at the other side the vision of the hospital-scene fading into the darkness, and already so faint that the furniture etc. behind are beginning to be visible through it.
[Inserted in No. 5. May 1856, with an illustration by Bennett as suggested.][123]

Ap: 14. (M). Mr. Jellinger Symons is still disputing the rotation of the moon, and begs for a rational proof. I have tried again (my first

---

122. *My Haunts and Their Frequenters* by Edmund Hodgson Yates (London: 1854).

123. Charles H. Bennett's illustration fits closely Dodgson's vision for the picture (see *The Train*, vol. 1 p. 287).

was not inserted). Went to the Bodleian to try and find out something of the genealogy of my great-grandfather, Bishop of Elphin. The extract on the opposite page is the result, and the line now reaches back to St. John's, Cambridge.[124]

[*Ossory*

1765. Charles Dodgson MA was an Englishman, educated at St. John's College, Cambridge. For some years he kept a school at Stanwix, Cumberland. He was Chaplain to the Duke of Northumberland, Lord Lieutenant. His patent is dated July 18th, and he was consecrated in St. Werburgh's Church, Dublin, on August 11th, by the Archbishop of Dublin, assisted by the Bishops of Kildare and Limerick. In 1775 he was translated to Elphin.

Elphin

1775. Charles Dodgson D.D. Bishop of Ossory, succeeded. His patent is dated

---

124. Charles Dodgson (1721-95), was Bishop of Elphin from 1775-95. For further details, see "Lewis Carroll and the Dodgson Lineage" by Philip Dodgson Jaques published in *Mr. Dodgson: Nine Lewis Carroll Studies* (The Lewis Carroll Society: 1973). The book which Dodgson consulted was *Fasti Ecclesiae Hibernicae. The succession of the prelates and members of the cathedral bodies in Ireland* by Henry Cotton, Dean of Lismore (Dublin: 1845-60 in 5 volumes). See also 19 and 21 February, above.

April 12th. He died in Dublin, on January 21st 1795, and was buried at St. Bridgets, in that city.

from Cotton's *Fasti Ecclesis Hibernico.*]

Ap: 15. (Tu). Found the titles of two sermons by the Bishop of Ossory in a Dictionary in the Library. The extract is given opposite. Dined with Fowler.

[Dodgson, Charles, Bishop of Ossory, Ireland. Sermon Prov: iii.27. 1761.4^{to} On Isai: lviii.6-8. 1768. 4to]

Ap: 16. (W). Walked with Otter and Ranken, and afterwards dined with the former.[125]

Ap: 23. (W). Heard Gavazzi lecture in the Town Hall on "Tractarianism":[126] very little could be heard, as the undergraduates present hooted and hissed a great part of the time.

---

125. Francis Otter matriculated at Corpus Christi College on 1 March 1850, aged 18, and was a scholar from 1850-61. He gained his B.A. in 1854. He was a Fellow from 1861-75, tutor in 1871 and held the post of Vice-President. In 1867, he became a barrister-at-law at Lincoln's Inn. Later in his career he became MP for Lincolnshire (Louth division), holding his parliamentary seat from December 1885 to June 1886.

126. Alessandro Gavazzi, Italian orator of the Risorgimento, who fled to England in 1849 and became associated with the Italian Protestants in London. He was declared a heretic for supporting a united Italy and for criticising the government of the Papal states.

Ince, one of the Proctors, made a speech from the platform to try to obtain order, but it had almost no effect.[127] The lecture was well delivered, but mere rhetorical nonsense in substance: he quoted (in order to refute) an argument for the Pope's infallibility, that he claims this on the ground of being called "Most Holy:" I doubt the argument ever having been seriously put forward.

Afterwards gave Scoltock a lesson in Euclid: he wishes to get it up again.

Ap: 24. (Th). Got a new bookcase into the little room, which I intend living in chiefly, reserving the large room for lectures.[128] Borrowed from Tyrwhitt two of his pen-and-ink sketches to copy. One is from Turner,

---

127. William Ince (1825-?), matriculated at Lincoln College in 1842; B.A. 1846; Fellow 1847-78; M.A. 1849; tutor 1850-78; sub-rector 1857-78; proctor 1856; D.D. at Christ Church by decree in 1878 when he became Regius Professor of Divinity and Canon at Christ Church.

128. Dodgson occupied room four above the Cloisters from 1852. This, in fact, consisted of two rooms, one of which was occupied by George Girdlestone Woodhouse, to whom Dodgson dedicated his poem, "The Ligniad." At the end of 1853 he moved next door to more spacious accommodation in room five, actually two main rooms as indicated here and probably additional bedrooms. His appointment as Mathematical Lecturer in the Autumn of 1855 probably gave rise to the designation of his larger room as a teaching space, reserving the smaller room for his living quarters. For more details of his college accommodation, see "Lewis Carroll's Rooms at Christ Church, Oxford" (*Jabberwocky*, vol. 12, no. 3: Summer 1983).

subject "Cephalus and Procris," and is a very striking and spirited sketch.

Ap: 25. (F).   Went over with Southey in the afternoon to the Deanery, to try and take a photograph of the Cathedral: both attempts proved failures. The three little girls were in the garden most of the time, and we became excellent friends: we tried to group them in the foreground of the picture, but they were not patient sitters. I mark this day with a white stone.[129]

Went to Scoltock in the evening to tea and Euclid: he offers to coach me in History in return, and I seriously am thinking of closing with it, and attacking my old enemy, Hume's *England*, again.[130]

Ap: 28. (M).   Deanery again in the afternoon. Southey tried the view of Merton from the walk

---

129.   Dodgson's first reference to Alice. He already knew Harry and Lorina Liddell. The three little girls where Lorina (Lina or Ina) Charlotte aged 6 (almost 7), Alice Pleasance aged 3 (almost 4), and Edith Mary (Tillie) aged 2. The fact that Dodgson marked the day with a white stone is significant here; meeting the children was more important to him than the photography which proved to be a failure.

130.   *The History of England* by David Hume (1711-76), numerous editions from 1754. Dodgson probably refers to *The History of England, from the Invasion of Julius Caesar to the end of the reign of George II. By Hume & Smollett. With the continuation from the accession of George III to the accession of Queen Victoria. By T. S. Hughes.* This was a new edition in 18 volumes (London: 1854-55).

before the house, a much more promising view as far as light goes, however all failed. The children were with us a good deal of the time. Boat races began.

Ap: 29. (Tu). Went over again with Southey to the Deanery about four, but all failed. Harry was with us most of the time, and Lina {Lorina} just at the end.

Ap: 30. (W). We went for the last time to the Deanery, and brought every thing away, to wait for better chemicals before trying again. We saw none of the family this time.

May 1. (Th). Had a party of tutors etc. to breakfast: I asked Marshall, Lloyd, Prout, Tyrwhitt, Bayne, Scoltock, Sandford, Rowley, the two Longley{s}, Joyce, and Southey. (Scoltock was asked to fill the place of Joyce, who is gone down).[131]

---

131.   The Christ Church Tutors were: George Marshall (1817-97) Examiner and Censor, Charles Lloyd (1824-62), Thomas Jones Prout (1823-1909), Richard St. John Tyrwhitt (1827-95), Thomas Vere Bayne (1829-1908), William Scoltock (1823-86), Charles Waldegrave Sandford (1828-1903), Richard Rowley (1832-64), Henry Longley (1832-99) and possibly his brother George Longley (1835-92), who may have been visiting after his service in the Crimean War (although he was not a scholar or tutor at Christ Church), Sidney Joyce (1834-1911), and Reginald Southey (1835-99). For Dodgson's photographic portraits of Prout, Sandford, Tyrwhitt, Bayne, Marshall, Henry Longley, and Joyce, see *Oxford Pamphlets*, pp. 13, 39, 178, 218, 236, and 286.

My camera arrived. Heard Lloyd preach on the Ascension at Ch. Ch.

Did some photographs with the spoiled collodium of Southey's, and afterwards sketched one of Tyrwhitt's pictures. I took it to show him, but he says I have worked on the wrong principle: the proper way is *to copy every single line.*

May 6. (Tu). The Dean sent for me to tell me he wishes me to read out the "Life" at the Gaudy this time. He chose "Richard Hakluyt," author of a book of travels.[132]

May 7. (W). Fletcher called in the middle of the day, and stayed about an hour:[133] he has come up for a day or two, and leaves today. Collyns arrived in the evening, and slept in the small bedroom: he stays till tomorrow.

[

]

---

132. Dodgson's "Life of Richard Hakluyt" was read in Hall at the Gaudy, a meeting of old members of Christ Church, on 31 May, and his manuscript survives to this day in the Library.

133. Charles Robert Fletcher Lutwidge (1835-1907), Dodgson's cousin (see *Diary 1*, p. 109 n. *125*). Dodgson also included in his journal some attempts at monograms on Fletcher's name.

1856

May 8. (Th). Heard from Woodhouse, accepting my offer of bed and board for his brother, who is going to try for one of the Slade scholarships.[134] Got some chemicals from London: 4 oz. iodised collodium; 2 oz. Glacial Acetic Acid; ½ oz. Pyro Gallic Acid. I spent the afternoon with Southey, photographing: he and I each took a portrait of Collyns, and, after several failures, he succeeded with my help in getting a good one of himself.

May 9. (F). Young Woodhouse arrived in the evening, and we went together to see the boat-races, the last night. We leave off fourth on the river.

May 10. (Sat). Spent a great part of the day photographing with Southey, or rather looking on. He took Faussett, Hewitt, Harington, myself etc.:[135] as it was so good a day for it, I went over to the Library, and called to Harry Liddell from

---

134. Charles Goddard Woodhouse, George Girdlestone Woodhouse's younger brother, arrived at Christ Church from Sedgeley, Staffordshire, in order to matriculate, which he succeeded in doing on 15 May. He gained his B.A. in 1860.

135. The subjects of the photographs were: Robert Godfrey Faussett (1827-1908), James Francis Katharinus Hewitt (1836-1908), and Richard Harington (1835-1911). For Dodgson's photographs of Faussett and Harington, see *Oxford Pamphlets*, pp. 239 and 286.

the window, and got him to come over to Southey's room.[136] We had great difficulty in getting him to sit still long enough: he succeeded at last, by placing him in a bright light, in getting a fair profile. Got my new picture over from Ryman's: "The Lovely Sisters" by Lawrence: it will make a good photograph.[137] Tyrwhitt proposes my trying some of his etchings.

[Mar. 23/66. Their name "Calmedy"]

I have been fitting up my small room under Scoltock's advice, and have already added a bookcase, 2 arm chairs, and a writing-table.

May 11.(Sun). Whitsunday. Heard the Bishop of Lincoln preach at St. Mary's.

May 12. (M). Asked Pickard to Common Room, and afterwards walked with him.[138]

---

136. The photograph of Harry Liddell in profile has not surfaced. Other photographs of Harry, taken by Dodgson, appear in an album at Princeton.

137. Sir Thomas Lawrence's picture of "The Lovely Sisters," engraved by Frederick Lewis, see n. *29* above. Dodgson's additional note for 23 March 1866, identifies Calmedy {sic} as the name of the sisters in the portrait which is listed as "The Calmady Children" in Bryan's *Biographical Dictionary of Painters and Engravers* (1904).

138. Henry Adair Pickard (1832-?), Student of Christ Church; see *Diary 1*, p. 84 n. *88*.

Ordered a small *gutta percha* bath, bottles, etc. at Telfer's.[139]

May 13. (Tu). Went to ask the Dean's permission to take one of my brothers into Frank's spare rooms, to take back the Slade papers, and to show him Harry's likeness and Southey's book of photographs: he asked me to stay luncheon, and Mrs. Liddell proposed to bring over Harry again: Southey agreed to try him, and got one tolerable picture and several failures. The party, consisting of Mrs. Liddell, her mother Mrs. Reeves, and Harry were over in Southey's rooms about an hour.[140]

Invitation to dine at the Deanery on Saturday next.

Southey spent a long time making up developing fluid etc. for me, so that I am now ready to begin the art. Breakfasted with Marshall.

May 14. (W). Spoke to the Dean about Woodhouse,

---

139. A bath made from the solidified juice of the gutta percha tree which produced gum with similar properties to rubber, although less elastic. This was probably used for developing photographs. The shop in Cornmarket Street was owned by Frederick Telfer who was a chemist and druggist. He was also an agent for the Yorkshire Fire and Life Office.

140. Southey's photograph of Harry Liddell has not surfaced (see n. *136* above). His grandmother was Lorina Reeve née Farr (?-1879) who married James Reeve (1777-1827), a landowner in Oulton, Suffolk.

who seems to have done very little in the examination, telling him also that Woodhouse thinks his name has been down for some years. We hunted the books, but it was not to be found, and at last sent off a telegraph message for further information to be sent by post. He moved to Brook's house, as Skeffington Hume and Wilfred Longley have arrived.[141] We called together on Halton of University, who asked us all to breakfast tomorrow morning.[142]

May 15. (Th). The elder Woodhouse arrived before breakfast to see about his brother, who at last got matriculated, chiefly owing to my undertaking to house him next term. I marked his Arithmetic paper "f.s.?" and my brothers' papers "sat" and "s.b."[143] Woodhouse Senior left in the evening.

---

141. George Brooks was Dodgson's scout and he lived at 48 St. Aldate's Street, very near to Christ Church.

142. John Foster Halton from Liverpool matriculated at University College in 1855 aged 18.

143. The coding Dodgson used when marking examination papers is not entirely clear. The initials may refer to Latin words; "f.s." probably stands for "fortiter satis" meaning "sufficient enough" (passable); "sat" stands for "satis" meaning "sufficient" (acceptable); and "s.b." stands for "satis bonus" meaning "sufficiently good" (good). Dodgson used other codes when marking papers such as "non suff", "malè" and "med" which probably stand for, respectively, "insufficient", "bad" and "middling"

Took several likenesses in the day, but all more or less failures.

May 16. (F). Mayo's younger brother called:[144] he has just rowed up to Oxford with a friend. My brothers left early in the morning, and young Woodhouse soon afterwards.

May 17. (Sat). Gave Mayo breakfast and lunch, at which Bailey and Milman joined us, we went down afterwards and saw the end of the Ch. Ch. and All England match.[145] We were beaten in one innings, with about 50 runs to spare. Dined at the Deanery in the evening, and met Bonamy Price (one of the former masters of Rugby).[146] In the evening was a large musical party, fair as far as music went, but too much crowded for enjoyment: I left about 11.

---

144. Robert Mayo's brother, Charles Thomas, does not appear to have attended Oxford University.

145. Alfred Bailey (1830-98) matriculated at Christ Church in 1847, gained his B.A. in 1851 and his M.A. in 1854. He became a barrister-at-law at Lincoln's Inn in 1854. Arthur Milman (1829-?) was a Westminster Student at Christ Church from 1846-60. He gained his B.A. in 1850 and his M.A. in 1853. He, too, became a barrister-at-law, but at the Inner Temple in 1853. He was commissary of the dean and chapter of St. Paul's, London, in 1869, and registrar of the University of London from 1879.

146. Bonamy Price (1807-88) took his M.A. at Worcester College in 1829, and went on to become a mathematics teacher at Rugby until 1850. Hence, he was there during Dodgson's time. He then became Drummond Professor of Political Economy at Oxford from 1868 until his death.

May 18.(Sun).I am getting into habits of unpunctuality, and must try to make a fresh start in activity: I record this resolution as a test for the future.

May 19. (M). The Dean came to the Library today, with Harry and Ina, to put books away. (The visitation is to be this day fortnight). Went down with Sandford to see the Oxford and Marylebone match.

May 20. (Tu). Walked over to Cuddesden with Liddon and Bellett to the Anniversary.[147] There was a cold collation, and a great deal of speech-making afterwards, from the Bishops of Oxford and Columbo. The Archdeacon of Berkshire, Liddon Senior, and Pott, and an American clergyman, I think of the name of Bewell. We left Oxford about half past 11 and got back about 7.

---

147.   Cuddesdon Theological College, opened in 1854 by Samuel Wilberforce, Bishop of Oxford, was the centre for candidates seeking ordination. The first Principal was the Rev. Alfred Potts. Dodgson did not enrol as a regular student at Cuddesdon, although he was in due course ordained there as Deacon of the Church of England on 22 December 1861. John Liddon (1835-?) and George Bellet (1833-86), two of Dodgson's mathematical undergraduates, joined him on this second anniversary celebrating the establishment of Cuddesdon. The senior Liddon, brother of John, was Dodgson's friend and travelling companion during the Russian tour, Henry Parry Liddon (1829-90), who was already making his mark as an influential speaker on theological topics. Liddon was the first Vice-Principal of Cuddesdon.

1856

Rowley went down the river with Harington (whose birthday it is), so that I had to miss the Library at my own risk.

May 21. (W). Breakfast with Lumsdaine.[148]

Received from my father a copy of his *Sermons on the Christian Sabbath*.[149]

Finished that extraordinary book *Wuthering Heights*:[150] it is of all novels I ever read the one I should least wish to be a character in myself. All the *dramatis personæ* are so unusual and unpleasant. The only failure in the book is the writing it in the person of a gentleman. Heathcliff and Catherine are original and most powerfully-drawn idealities: one cannot believe that such human beings ever existed: they have far more of the fiend in them. The vision at the beginning is I

---

148. Francis Gordon Sandys Lumsdaine (1828-73) matriculated at Christ Church from Rugby School in 1846. He was a Student from 1847-57. He gained his B.A. in 1850 and his M.A. in 1853.

149. Archdeacon Charles Dodgson published a number of religious books and sermons. The gift to his son was probably *The Sabbath, a delight*. A sermon published in 1840 as part of a compilation of sermons edited by George Dugard and Alexander Watson under the title, *Sermons by XXXIX living divines of the Church of England* (London: 1840).

150. *Wuthering Heights. A Novel, by Ellis Bell* published in 1847 in two volumes. The authoress was Emily Jane Brontë (1818-48).

think the finest piece of writing in the book.

May 22. (Th). Borrowed a catalogue of the R.A. from Rowley to look over, and made a list of some that seemed worth notice.
[54, 62, 67, 75, 94, 192, 200, 208, 259, 273, 299, 327, 352, 448, 530, 310, 413, 532, 553, 559, 587, 810, 873, 896, 907, 919, 938, 1002, 1310.][151]

---

151.   The catalogue in question is the 88th Annual Exhibition of the Royal Academy of Arts (1856). The titles of the pictures which Dodgson thought worthy of notice were as follows: 54: *The administration of the Lord's Supper* by J. C. Horsley; 62: *Charles Dickens, Esq.* by A. Scheffer; 67: *The Lady Edith Campbell and the Lord George Campbell, children of His Grace the Duke of Argyll* by J. Sant; 75: *The last parting of Marie Antoinette and her son* by E. M. Ward; 94: *The abandoned* by C. Stanfield; 192: *View near Oxford* by H. Ash; 200: *Peace concluded, 1856* by J. E. Millais; 208: *Highland nurses* (dedicated to Miss Nightingale) by Sir E. Landseer; 259: *"On the look out"* by H. Le Jeune; 273: *Home and the homeless* by T. Faed; 299: *A Lancashire witch, residing at Bolton-le-Sands* by J. C. Horsley; 327: *The children in the wood* by J. Sant; 352: *Chatterton* by H. Wallis; 448: *Autumn leaves* by J. E. Millais; 530: *An April afternoon at Easby Abbey* by J. Peel; 310: *The parable of the children in the market-place* by W. T. C. Dobson; 413: *A wounded cavalier* by W. S. Burton; 532: *The prosperous days of Job* by W. T. C. Dobson; 553: *L'Enfant du Régiment* by J. E. Millais; 559: *The pet's pet* by J. Sant; 587: *Byron's early love* by E. M. Ward; 810: *Master Henry Kemble, grandson of the late Charles Kemble, Esq.* by Miss A Liberty; 873: *View from the Mount of Offence, looking towards the Dead Sea and the Mountains of Moab - morning* by W. Holman Hunt; 896: *Miss Harriet Dickens* by Miss J. S. Egerton; 907: *Mrs. Coventry Patmore* by J. Brett; 919: *Mrs. Charles Kingsley* by E. Havell; 938: *Sons of the Rev. J. P. Marriott* by J. C. Moore; 1002: *The Sphinx, Gizeh, looking towards the pyramids of Sakhara* by W. Holman Hunt; and 1310: *Charles Kean, Esq., in the character of Wolsey* by E. G. Papworth.

May 23. (F). Began going over the books in the Library for the Visitation.

May 27. (Tu). Spent most of the evening in drawing up an arranged list of the events in the life of Hakluyt, and wrote a conclusion for it.

May 29. (Th). Sat up late, writing Hakluyt's life: about half past one in the morning the men began to explode fireworks in Chaplain's Quadrangle, and three of them came out and threw bottles into Lloyd's windows. I went over to Lloyd's rooms and woke him: he got up and dressed and went over for Marshall: we went into Page's rooms, from which we saw the last fireworks come, but the offenders had beat a retreat.[152]

May 30. (F). The last day of Collections. Finished Hakluyt's life.

May 31. (Sat). Spent the day in the Library: read out the life in Hall, and afterwards dined at the

---

152.   The east and south ranges of the Chaplain's Quadrangle were demolished in 1863 to make way for the new Meadow Buildings. Charles Lloyd, who was then a Student at Christ Church, shared some of the mathematical tutoring with Dodgson. George Marshall was Censor at Christ Church and had responsibility for discipline within the college. Herbert William Cobbold Page, an undergraduate, was clearly not occupying his rooms at the time, and these had been used by persons unknown to launch fireworks.

> high table: the noise was tremendous, and Gordon turned several men out of Hall.

June 2. (M). Library visitation, no books missing. Boat. Procession at night.

June 3. (Tu). Spent the morning at the Deanery, photographing the children. In the afternoon went with Liddon to the Horticultural Show in Worcester Gardens. Afterwards Frank and I, with Harry Liddell, went down to Sandford in a gig. We rowed with sculls down with Harry as stroke, and he steered back.

June 4. (W). Commemoration, which I did not attend.[153] Illumination at night: it was {an} interesting sight, as there was every variety of the thing to be seen, from gorgeous devices down to dip-candles. A fellow of Queen's, Jex-Blake,[154] had one

---

153.   Commemoration is the annual festival celebrating the founders and benefactors of the University, sometimes called the Encænia. The main event is held at the Sheldonian Theatre with speeches and recitals. The availability of fireworks to mark the celebrations may have resulted in the events which occurred during the evening of 29 May .

154.   Thomas William Jex-Blake (1832-?) matriculated at University College in 1851. He became a fellow of Queen's College from 1855-8. He took his M.A. in 1857 and his B. & D.D. in 1873. He became assistant master at Rugby School 1858-68 and Principal of Cheltenham College 1868-74. He returned to Rugby as headmaster in 1874. From 1886 he was rector of Alvechurch.

1856

eye blinded by a Roman Candle, and it is feared he may lose the other also. Ch. Ch. chiefly distinguished itself in fireworks, which the Dean had authorised and allowed men to go on the roofs to throw them.

June 5. (Th). Met an old school friend whom I have not seen for 10 years, Mounsey, who was at Richmond with me.[155] He came to my rooms to find me, but neither of us in the least recognised one another: we went together to his lodgings to see his sister, who is staying in Oxford with him, and I afterwards spent the evening with them, when we settled plans for lionising tomorrow.

In the interval, from half past four to seven, Frank and I made a boating excursion with Harry and Ina: the latter, much to my surprise, having got permission from the Dean to come. We went down to the island, and made a kind of picnic there, taking biscuits with us, and buying gingerbeer and lemonade there. Harry as before rowed stroke most of the way, and fortunately, considering

---

155. Dodgson did not meet Mounsey, his schoolboy acquaintance at Richmond School, for over a decade, hence it was hardly surprising that they did not recognise each other.

the wild spirits of the children, we got home without accident, having attracted by our remarkable crew a good deal of attention from almost every one we met. Mark this day, Annalist, not only with a white stone, but as altogether *dies mirabilis*. (In the morning I was introduced to Sir Edmund Lyons,[156] by Ogilvie,[157] who bought him to the Library).

June 6. (F). Mounsey and his sister came to luncheon, and we afterwards went over the Library. Bosanquet dined in Hall, having come over for a few hours.

June 7. (Sat). Spent the morning in paying bills. Called at the Deanery in the afternoon, and took tea with the Mounseys. Left Oxford by the 8.35 and reached Putney about 12.30.

---

156. Admiral Sir Edmund Lyons G.C.B. (1790-1858) was a graduate of Christ Church who took his M.A. in 1838. He was minister plenipotentiary at Athens. He was knighted in 1835, being at the time vice-admiral of the White. He was created a baronet in 1840. For his services in the Crimea he was created D.C.L. on 4 June (the previous day), and Baron Lyons a few days later, on 23 June.

157. Charles Atmore Ogilvie (1793-1873), Regius Professor of Pastoral Theology from 1842 and Canon of Christ Church from 1849. He was a graduate of Balliol, tutor (1819-30), bursar catechetical in 1822, and later senior dean. He was also vicar of Ross-on-Wye, Herefordshire, from 1839 until his death.

1856

Long Vacation

June 8. (Sun). I can see no change in the party here, except that Amy seems to have grown a little. Frank arrived yesterday, very lame, having given up his attempt at walking up to London at High Wickham.

June 9. (M). Went up to town, to see about the lens etc.

June 10. (Tu). Went up with Aunt Caroline and Lucy to the Water-Colour Exhibition, and afterwards by myself to the R.A. for about one and a half hours. In the evening with Frank to the Adelphi. We saw *The Flying Dutchman*, *A Bottle of Smoke*, and *Good Night Signor Pantalon*, in the first two of which Wright acted.[158] I thought him very good, but most of the acting poor, and some decidedly bad: the plot of the principal piece was confused to the last degree, a sort of mixture of drama and pantomime.

---

158. *The Flying Dutchman* was a nautical melodrama in three acts by Edward Fitzball (1782-1873). *A Bottle of Smoke* was an anonymous farce. *Goodnight Signior Pantalon* was a comic opera in one act based on Oxenford's *Twice Killed*. The actor was Edward Richard Wright (1813-59), best known for playing comic roles.

June 11. (W). Went to a school-feast given in the Bullars' garden, about 250 children were present and a number of visitors. The affair lasted about four hours, and went off most successfully: the children seemed wonderfully well behaved.[159]

June 12. (Th). A miscellaneous sort of party began about three: the day was to have been spent in hay-making, but turned out too rainy. Games etc. indoors were resorted to. I proposed a story-charade, which was tolerably successful: I took the old word "Fair-eye," the actors were Percy, Amy, Marla, Katty, Mary and Maggie Lockhart, Katie Murdoch, Gemma Adams, Edith Bullar and myself.[160] Afterwards there was a kind of dance among the children. The other guests were Charles, Minnie and the youngest Murdoch, David Bea, Charlie and Miss Lockhart, Mary and Ludovic Unwin, Arthur Walpole, and

---

159.   The Bullars lived at Fairfax House, 70 High Street, Putney. John Bullar (1807-?), a barrister with practices at Southampton and Temple, London, which he shared with his brother, Henry Bullar (1815-?), who was unmarried and lived with the family. John Bullar married Rosa Follett (1818-?) circa 1838 and they had at least four children; Suzanna Rosa F. A. (born 1839), Anne Mary (born 1841), Edith F. (born 1844) and Anna Katharine "Katty" (born 1847).

160.   Percy, Amy and Marla (Menella) were cousins, children of Uncle Hassard. Mary and Maggie Lockhart and Gemma Adams were family friends, so too was Katherine "Katie" Murdoch (?-1926).

Rosa and Mary Bullar.[161]

June 13. (F).   In the evening to the Olympic with Uncle
Hassard, Frank, and Percy. Robson acted
in one piece, and Wigan in one: Emery in
all. I never saw any of these before, and
thought them all excellent. Robson seems
to me to rant in some parts, and in others
to burlesque Kean: but he has the making
of a great actor. The pieces were *A
Fascinating Individual, Retribution* and
Stay at Home.[162]

June 16. (M).   To the Princess' with Frank. *Winter's Tale*

---

161.   Charles Stewart Murdoch, Millicent (Minnie) Horatia Murdoch and
possibly the youngest member of the family was Alice Maria Murdoch
(1852-81). For more on the Murdochs, see *Letters*, p. 33 n. *1*. For details
of Edith, Rosa and Mary Bullar, see n. *159* above. The other children
present are not identified, but were presumably friends of the Dodgsons at
Putney.

162.   Thomas Frederick Robson (1822-64), manager of the Olympic, showed
remarkable power in burlesque, farce, and serious parts. Dodgson saw him
perform many times at the Olympic and grew to admire his acting ability.
Horace Wigan (1818-85), comic actor, succeeded Robson at the Olympic.
He was the original "Hawkshaw" in Tom Taylor's *Ticket-of-Leave Man* in
1863. Samuel Anderson Emery (1817-81) excelled in the parts of old men
and rustics; he appeared in many dramatisations of Dickens's novels,
"Captain Cuttle" being his most famous role. *A Fascinating Individual*
was a one-act farce by Henry Danvers. *Retribution* was a domestic drama
by Tom Taylor (1817-80) founded on Charles de Bernard's novel, *La Loi
du Talion*. *Stay at Home* was a farce by George Henry Lewes (1817-78)
who also wrote under the pseudonym, Slingsby Lawrence.

preceded by *A Prince for an Hour*.[163] The farce was fair. The play not equal to *Henry VIII*, the visions were gorgeous, but did not please me nearly as much as Queen Catherine's dream. The concluding scene, of the statue of Hermione, was the most beautiful. I especially admired the acting of little Mamillius, Ellen Terry, a beautiful little creature, who played with remarkable ease and spirit.[164]

June 18. (W). Went to Brompton to breakfast with Uncle Skeffington, and afterwards paid a second visit to the Royal Academy. Uncle Skeffington dined with us at Putney. Called on Mr. Toynbee, the aurist.[165]

June 19. (Th). The Murdochs were brought over in the afternoon to be photographed, and stayed for the evening: their elder brother

---

163.   *A Prince for an Hour* was a comedy-drama in one act by John Maddison Morton (1811-91).

164.   Ellen Terry (1847-1928), in the role as Mamillius in *The Winter's Tale*, made her first appearance on stage when she was nine years old. Her début took place on 28 April. A photograph of her taken two days previously, with Charles Kean, is in the archives of the Theatre Museum, London. Charles Kean (1811-68) played Leontes, and Mrs. Kean played Hermione.

165.   Joseph Toynbee (1815-66) was one of the greatest aural surgeons of the 19th century. He was not able to cure Dodgson's deafness in his right ear.

1856

Charles came to dinner.[166]

June 20. (F). Left for Croft, where I arrived about half past eight in the evening. I heard the other day from Mr. Yates, saying that he has had an interview with Arnold and hopes to be able to arrange for having some of his writings in the *Train.* (Arnold proposed to try an essay on Hypatia, and another descriptive of Oxford life).[167]

June 26. (Th). Dined with Mr. Smith at Dinsdale.[168] Mr. Baker and I went in a fly together. Met a Mr. and Mrs. Brown, and a Major Grey, both relations of the family. Spent most of the evening with the children who have

---

166. Dodgson's photograph of Alice Murdoch is one of the earliest to survive. It is reproduced in Gernsheim's *Lewis Carroll, Photographer,* (Max Parrish: 1949), plate 5. See n. *161* above.

167. Frederick Arnold (see n. *100* above) contributed "Edmund Hyde, Lord Clarendon" to volume 2 of *The Train.* Nothing about Hypatia was included in any volume, nor any description of Oxford life.

168. John William Grey (1811-97) took the sole surname, Smith, by Royal Licence in 1833. He was the third son of William Grey J.P., and his wife Joanna née Scurfield; educated at Durham and Jesus College, Cambridge; B.A. 1834; M.A. 1837; curate of Dinsdale 1851-9; rector there until his death. He married Maria (1808-98), daughter of Lieut. Col. Thomas Robinson Grey of Norton on Tees, and his wife Elizabeth née Hogg, in 1839 and they had six children; Maria Grey (born 1843), Joanna Grey (1845-1932), Fanny Grey (1847-74), Anne Grey (born 1848) and William Arthur Grey (born 1850). The sixth child, Frederick John Grey, was born in 1853 but died in infancy. Dodgson's photographs of the Smith family feature in an album at Princeton.

grown out of my recollection. There names are most unpoetical; Maria, Johanna, Fanny and Ann, the youngest is a boy, I think Arthur.[169]

    Mrs. Nichol arrived in the evening.[170]

June 29. (F). Some of the party returned from the Lakes, Frances Jane, Elizabeth Lucy, and Skeffington Hume.

June 30. (M). Wrote to William Wilcox to know when I had better come over, also to Mr. Bainbridge, mentioning my intention of visiting Whitby some time this summer, also to Brooks, my scout, to ask him to enquire about rooms for my brothers and Woodhouse Junior.

July 1. (Tu). Walked over with Skeffington Hume to Dinsdale and called at the Smiths. I took some of my photographs to show them and arranged that a party of them are to come on Friday to sit.

---

169. Dodgson's travelling companion was James Baker, curate at Croft (see n. *119* above). Mr. and Mrs. Brown, related to the Smiths, are not identified. The relationship of Major Grey to the family has also not been identified. He is not Smith's father-in-law who was dead by this time.

170. Mrs. Nichol is possibly Charlotte Nichol née Hume (1807-?), wife of Dr. W. Nichol, and sister of Caroline Hume who married Dodgson's Uncle Hassard.

July 2. (W).   An expedition to Richmond. I took a part of the party up the bed of the "Hypanis." We called at the Ottleys before leaving, and found Mrs. Ottley at home, and four children: two boys, John and Lawrence, and two very odd little girls, Georgina and Agnes.[171]

July 7. (M).   Went over to Whitburn in the afternoon: found the party little altered, all but Ernest, who is very much what Charley used to be, talkative and friendly, but quaint.[172]

July 8. (Tu).   James Tate came over from Roker, where

---

171.   Lawrence Ottley (1808-61), rector of Richmond, canon and rural dean of Ripon, and his wife Elizabeth (1817-1902), née Bickersteth (sister of the Bishop of Ripon), had twelve children; Sarah "Sallie" (born 1836), Emily "Emmie" (1838-93), Portia (1839, died in infancy), Alice (1840-1912), Sophie Elizabeth "Bessie" (1841-54), Richard (1842, died in infancy), Lawrence "Lawrie" (born 1843), John Bickersteth (born 1845), Georgiana (born 1847), Agnes "Aggie" (born 1849), Henry "Harry" Bickersteth (1850-1932), Edward "Teddie" Bickersteth (1852-1910), Constance "Cooie" (1854-57), Robert "Robin" (born 1856), Charles "Charlie" (born 1858) and Herbert (born 1859). Alice became headmistress of Worcester High School which was eventually called "The Alice Ottley School." Dodgson visited the school on 28 November 1892, see *Letters* p. 933. Henry Bickersteth became a vicar at Eastbourne; Robert became a Canon of Christ Church and Regius Professor of Theology; and Charles became Admiral Sir Charles Ottley. The Dodgson sisters became very attached to the Ottleys. When the father died, Alice and Robert stayed with the Dodgsons at Croft for two weeks while Richmond Rectory was cleared. Alice also visited the Dodgson sisters at Guildford in 1869.

172.   Ernest Shepley Wilcox (1854-1926) and Charles Hassard Wilcox (1852-74) were Dodgson's cousins.

the party are staying. We went over there in the evening.[173]

July 9. (W).   Went to tea to Roker in the evening, and heard the band play: I never heard "Glorious Apollo" before, and liked it very much.[174] Met a Miss Bulman there, who is staying with her cousins, the Robinsons, and the Robinson party.[175]

July 11. (F).   Heard from Mounsey, enclosing two papers for the *Train*, "On the singularity of animals having only one Tail," and a poem on a little Highland girl. (He had before this sent me at my request another piece, which I thought would not do and so did not forward). I liked both, and returned them for correction, and wrote to

---

173.   James Tate (1835-?), son of Rev. James Tate (1801-63), Dodgson's headteacher at Richmond School. He matriculated at Corpus Christi, Oxford, in 1854, B.A. in 1858, ordained in 1863, and went on to become perpetual curate of Richmond Holy Trinity, later Rector of Plaxtol, Kent. See also n. *178* below.

174.   *Glorious Apollo, A Glee for Three Voices* composed by Samuel Webbe the Elder, edited with an accompaniment for piano by Sir Henry R. Bishop (1855). The original glee was composed for the London Glee Club in 1787.

175.   The Robinson family possibly descend from either James Septimus Robinson of Tunstall Lodge, Sunderland, or William Robinson Robinson of Silksworth Hall. However, a search of various directories and the census returns for 1851 and 1861 have failed to link them with the Bulman family. Bulman and Dixon were shipbrokers in Sunderland.

tell Mr. Yates to expect them.[176]

The Tates came over to be photographed: afterwards I read aloud *Done Brown*,[177] which was followed by a story-charade, in which Lucy Tate, William, Katie, Georgie, Lucy and I appeared, "Win-dough." [178]

July 12. (Sat). Returned to Croft.

While at Whitburn I heard from Mrs. Bainbridge, in answer to my letter to Lieutenant Bainbridge, saying that she is not thinking of leaving Whitby this summer, so that whenever I visit Whitby, I shall be sure to see them. Mr. Bainbridge is now at Balaclava, superintending the transporting of troops; he expects to be home in August.

July 19. (Sat). William Wilcox came over to stay two or

---

176.   Neither of Mounsey's contributions appear to have inspired Edmund Yates; they were not included in any issue of *The Train*.

177.   *Done Brown*, a farce by Henry Thornton Craven (1818-1905) which Dodgson saw performed at the Lyceum, Sunderland, on 21 September 1855. (see *Diary 1* for that date).

178.   Lucy Hutchinson Tate (born 1843), daughter of James Tate. Other members of the Tate family were: Ellen (born 1833), James (born 1835), Charles Grey (born 1836), Thomas Hutchinson (born 1837) and John Samuel (born 1840), but some of these had left home by this time. William, Katherine (Katy), Elizabeth Georgina (Georgie), and Isabella Lucy were all Wilcox cousins. See *Diary 1*, p. 124 n. *154*.

three days: he wishes to see some photographic printing, in which accordingly we spent the day.

July 23. (W). William returned to Whitburn: wrote the second part of "The Three Voices" into *Mischmasch*. I am thinking of sending it to Yates as an experiment. (see Oct: 7).[179]

July 24. (Th). Began regular work, and read for an hour or two. I am taking up Italian and Natural Botany as πἀρεργα to the real work.[180]

Aug: 12 (Tu). Left Croft with Skeffington Hume and Wilfred Longley for Keswick, to meet Collyns there on Friday. We travelled from Penrith by coach: Skeffington and I during the last part of the journey were perched on the top of the luggage. We reached Mr. Webster's about eight. He has a new pupil of the name of Cross, and besides him we found there a scholar of Trinity, Paisley, and a youth of the name

---

179. The version of "The Three Voices" written into *Mischmasch* with Dodgson's own illustrations was revised for inclusion in *The Train* where it appeared in volume 2, pp. 278-84 without illustration. The poem was extensively altered and added to when it appeared in *Phantasmagoria* (1869) and *Rhyme? and Reason?* (1883), the latter version illustrated by Arthur Frost. The poem describes a feeble man distracted by a powerful and overbearing woman, in a parody of Tennyson's *Two Voices*.

180. The Greek translates: "unessential"

1856

Campbell with a Mrs. Pattinson, (the two last are staying in Portinscale a day or two).[181] I could not see in the mountains as much grandeur as I expected: to appreciate them properly, one ought to have heard nothing about them before.

Aug: 13. (W). Did a few photographs in the morning, and rowed on the lake for an hour with Skeffington Hume and Campbell to steer.[182] Walked into Keswick and bought a knapsack and waterproof coat. Called

---

181.   Alexander Rhind Webster (1816-90?), was born in Scotland, the son of Andrew and Anne Webster of St. Andrews. He was educated at St Mary Hall, Oxford; B.A. 1841; M.A. 1844; curate at South Luffenham, Rutland (1841-3); perpetual curate at Bothamstall, Notts., and chaplain to the Duke of Newcastle (1843-6); perpetual curate at Bradninch, Devon (1846-53); rural dean (1849-55); curate at Croft (1853-55) for Charles Dodgson senior; curate at Crosthwaite, Cumberland (1855-63); rector of Ilketshall, Suffolk (1863-5); vicar at Chatham, Kent (1865-8); and vicar at Addingham, Cumberland (1868-73). He was inspector of schools for the Diocese of Carlisle in 1869. He was also the author of several school text books of Latin and Greek Classics. Eventually he became rector of Tinwell, Rutland in 1884. While he was curate at Crosthwaite, Webster apparently ran a summer school at Keswick for students preparing to enter Oxford University. He was married with four children; the two daughters that Dodgson met on his visit were Charlotte Augusta (born 1847) and Mary Elizabeth (born 1849). His pupils were, possibly, John Henry Cross, a student at Trinity College; B.A. 1860; M.A. 1863, and Claud Campbell, another scholar who matriculated at Trinity College in December 1858 at the age of 18, who went on to gain his B.A. in 1862 and M.A. in 1865. Paisley and Mrs Pattinson, are not identified. Dodgson's photographs of the Websters survive in an album at Princeton.

182.   Dodgson's photographs of the Lake District. taken at this time, are included in album VI (see Gernsheim, p. 98).

on Mrs. Favell.[183]

Aug: 14. (Th). Heavy rain a great part of the day. Went with Mr. Webster to the Favells, where I remained and spent the evening.

Aug: 15. (F). Went with Skeffington Hume to near the foot of Dodd in the evening.

Aug: 16.(Sat). Photographed all the morning. In the afternoon Mr. Webster, Skeffington Hume and I were going with the two little girls to take the Church and Southey's monument, but it turned out too dull to photograph, and as Mr. Webster was detained by business we went a walk with the children instead: up Castlet, and thence on to Friar's Cray. In the afternoon I was introduced by Mr. Webster to Wordsworth's eldest son and his wife who happened to call.[184]

Collyns arrived at Keswick late in the evening.

---

183.   Anne Elizabeth Favell (1789-1871), daughter of Cornelius Cayley and his wife Sarah née Ward, married James Favell, a widower, in 1828 at Sowerby by Thirsk. They lived at Derwent Lodge, Portinscale.

184.   William Wordsworth (1770-1850) married Mary Hutchinson in 1802 and settled at Dove Cottage, Grasmere. There were five children; John (born 1803), Dora (1804-47), Thomas (1806-12), Catherine (1808-12) and William (born 1810).

1856

Aug: 18. (M). Collyns and I started on our walking tour: Mr. Webster, with Skeffington and a pupil of the name of Benn, accompanied us most of the day. We began by rowing down to Lowdore; then, without stopping to look at the falls there, which are nearly empty, we walked down Borrowdale, and lunched at Seathwaite, where it is said more rain falls in the year than in any other place in England. The whole party ascended Great Gable, but we got no view, as it was entirely wrapped up in mists. At the foot the party divided, and Collyns and I walked on to Wasthead, where we got beds at a cottage.

Aug: 19. (Tu). Today we walked on to St. Bees, and lunched at Calder Bridge on the way, after which we went to look at the Abbey there: the ruins are fine, but there is very little left of them. Before leaving Wasthead, we measured the little church there: it is 37 feet long, 19 broad, and 5 feet high up to the eaves: all outside measurement.

At Gosforth, which we passed on the way, we noticed a curious old cross in the churchyard: it consists of a square pillar, carved all over, 12 or 15 feet high: this gradually tapers upwards, and at the top there is a perfect Maltese cross, joined with a circle.

As far as Calder Bridge the views were most beautiful: after that the country is flat and uninteresting.

Aug: 20. (W). Before leaving St. Bees we went over the church, and had a long search after the college buildings, which I firmly believed to exist. All there is of the kind is a sort of room for Divinity lectures, and this they have got by appropriating the chancel: the students all lodge in the town.

There is a curious inscription, in base-relief, in the vestry at St. Bees.

[

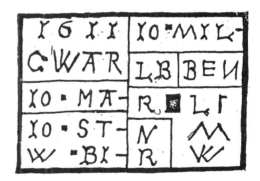

]

On our way thence to Ennerdale we fell in with a Mr. Ainger, a resident of St. Bees, who advised us to go from Ennerdale to Buttermere over Red Pike: however we managed to miss the way, and ascended Starling Dodd instead: this is next to Red Pike, and Scale Force runs out between them.[185]

Aug: 21. (Th). From Buttermere round by the Vale of Lorton and Whinlatter to Portinscale again. We came out upon the view of Bassenthwaite in time to see a magnificent effect on the opposite side of the valley. A thick curtain of mist was drawing slowly up the mountain side, leaving the valley below in bright sunlight; and in the mist against the mountain lay a rainbow, which reached nearly all the way from Bassenthwaite to Derwentwater.

We took our roadside lunch for the last time at Braithwaite, and reached Portinscale about four in the afternoon.

Aug: 22. (F). In the afternoon Collyns and I rowed down to Herbert's Island, taking Charlotte and Mary with us. It was I think the most

---

185. George Henry Ainger (1819-86), born St. Bees, only son of Rev. William Ainger, perpetual curate and first Principal of St. Bees Theological College, and his wife Elizabeth née Humphries; educated at Sedbergh and St. Johns, Camb.; B.A. 1842; M.A. 1845, D.D. 1859; ordained priest 1846; curate Alford Som. 1847-8; tutor St. Bees College, Cum. 1849-57; Principal and perpetual curate at St. Bees 1858-70; rector of Rothbury, Northumberland, until his death. Buried at St. Bees; East window in All Saints Rothbury to his memory. He was Hon. Canon of Carlisle 1870-82, and Newcastle 1880-6; a proctor in Convocation and a rural dean. He married Eliza Janet Hodgson in 1850. There were nine children.

perfectly lovely day I ever saw, and the water as smooth as glass: I never enjoyed rowing more thoroughly. The little girls rowed us a part of the way, and steered the rest.

Aug: 23.(Sat). Collyns ascended Skiddaw with Skeffington. I was prevented going by a swelled face, the result of the ascent of Great Gable, and the icy cold wind we met at the top.

Aug: 26. (Tu). Our plan was to go to Ambleside by the afternoon coach, and I had written to Uncle Henry to tell him of our coming, and engaged places on the coach.[186] Collyns walked on in the morning with Skeffington, and ascended Helvellyn, and I was to follow by coach and join him at Wyburn, but the pain in my face prevented me. I sent him a note by the coach enclosing one to Uncle Henry, and forwarded his luggage (as there was no room for it on the coach), by a return carriage. He met the coach, and not finding his luggage thereon, walked back to Portinscale, and sent on the enclosed note to Ambleside, thus making up a

---

186.   Commander Henry Thomas Lutwidge, R.N. (1786-?), Dodgson's great-uncle on his mother's side.

regular system of cross-purposes. To mend the matter, our lodging-house keeper, Mrs. Knubbley,[187] had carefully directed all his luggage to Captain Lutwidge, which (as we have not yet been offered beds there) will probably produce some confusion there, arising as it will without an owner, but *with* a letter of introduction!

Aug: 27. (W). We came on by coach and reached Ambleside without further complication. We found there Uncle and Aunt Lutwidge, Henry, Anna, and Mary Poole.[188] After luncheon we walked along the side of Windermere: in the evening Henry Poole showed us some interesting drawings of mining machinery in America, and some ground plans and elevations of which he took in the Holy Land. These inspired me with two new ideas, both of which I hope to carry out: to collect ground plans of English Abbeys

---

187.   Margaret Knubley (1816-65), wife of Richard Knubley, a master carpenter. They had one son named Lupton Knubley (born 1846). Mrs Knubley lived in Portinscale and accommodated visitors.

188.   Henry Thomas Lutwidge married Mary, daughter of John Taylor of Townhead, Lancashire. She was Dodgson's great-aunt. Henry, Anna and Mary were the children of Henry's sister, Henrietta Octavia Poole, née Lutwidge, who had married Charles Poole (1758-1838) of Stanmore in 1801. Henrietta Poole died in 1848.

and other ruins, and to make a Long Vacation tour to the Holy Land: the latter would be far more enjoyable if I could only manage to carry my Photography with me.[189]

Aug: 28. (Th). It rained nearly all day, and at last, in despair of better weather, we sallied out in waterproofs to look at Rydel Falls: they are not imposing, either in height or breadth; the scenery around is beautiful.

Aug: 29. (F). Collyns set off to walk to Penrith: I remained to take some photographs, and followed by train. Fowler fell in with Collyns at the "Crown," and the two had walked out when I arrived to escape the society of two Americans in the coffee-room: their insufferable vulgarity and overbearing manner was too disagreeable to be amusing, and we retired early, and spent the rest of the evening in one of our bedrooms. Fowler intends going on tomorrow into Scotland.

Aug: 30.(Sat). We set out by coach for Barnard Castle at about seven, and passed over about 40 miles of the dreariest hill country I ever saw: the climax of wretchedness was

---

189.   Dodgson's proposed trip to the Holy Land did not materialise.

reached in Bowes, where yet stands the original of Dickens' "Dotheboy's Hall": it has long ceased to be used as a school, and is falling into ruin, in which the whole place seems to be following its example, the roofs are falling in, and the windows broken or barricaded, the whole town looks plague-stricken. The courtyard of the inn we stopped at was grown over with weeds, and a mouthing idiot lolled against the corner of the house, like the evil genius of the spot. Next to a prison or a lunatic-asylum, preserve me from living at Bowes!

We stayed to visit Barnard Castle, with its exceedingly objectionable guide in the form of a hermit, who decoyed us into his cell, where he had two or three other victims waiting, seated himself gravely at the other end of the room, and, after a solemn pause to prepare us, began repeating, in a dead monotone, a sort of history of the place. I was immediately seized with a fit of laughter, which I only just succeeded in stifling, and sat for 10 minutes or more, looking fixedly out of the window, in a state of agony, and longing for escape. We seized on the opportunity of the first pause he made to fee him and take our departure: the relief of getting into the garden was indescribable, we almost lay down and rolled, I think he must have heard our shouts of laughter, all the more violent from being pent up so long.

We went on by railway, and reached Croft without further adventure.

Aug: 31.(Sun).Took Collyns up Stapleton and Eryholme banks etc.

Sep: 1. (M).   Collyns and I went over and lionised Richmond. Bought *Dred.*[190]

Sep: 5. (F).   Finished "Upon the lonely moor," (a parody on Wordsworth's poem about the leech gatherer), and sent it off to Yates on the chance of its suiting for "The Waiting Room." [191]
[Inserted in No. 10, October 1856.]

Sep: 12. (F).   Finished and sent off to Yates "Novelty and Romancement," at the same time suggesting a concluding vignette, a signboard hanging against a wall, with a broken window or two in sight to carry

---

190.   *Dred; A Tale of the Great Dismal Swamp* by Harriet Beecher Stowe (1811-96), was published in 1856 in Boston. She was also the authoress of *Uncle Tom's Cabin* (1852). Both books had anti-slavery themes.

191.   "The Waiting Room," at the end of each issue of *The Train,* contained shorter contributions. "Upon the Lonely Moor" appeared anonymously in the second volume of *The Train,* pp. 255-6, and is a parody of Wordsworth's "Resolution and Independence." Dodgson revised the poem and used it as the White Knight's song in *Looking-Glass.*

out the idea of desolation.[192]

[see Jan: 21. Inserted in No. 10 with an illustration as suggested, by McConnell.]

Sep: 16. (Tu). Went over to Whitburn with Mary and Louisa. Arthur Wilcox arrived at Croft (for a week's stay) just before we left. We were fortunate enough to come in for a concert in the schoolroom for the benefit of the Mechanics' Institute. Lady Williamson sang a good deal; the rest was by the Sunderland choral society.[193]

We had the music in *Macbeth*, *Bonnie Prince Charlie* (Lady W.), *The Chorister Crow*, *Wanted a Governess* (one of Patey's {?} songs) and as the encore to it *The King of Otaheiti*, *My hearts in the Hielands* (Lady W.) and as its encore *Merry Saviss boy*, *March of the*

---

192.   Dodgson's narrative "Novelty and Romancement. A Broken Spell" was published in the second volume of *The Train*, pp. 249-54, and contains an illustration as described, drawn by William McConnell.

193.   Dodgson probably realised that Lady Williamson was Dean Liddell's cousin. She was the third daughter of Thomas Henry Liddell (1775-1855), First Lord Ravensworth, and his wife Maria Susannah Simpson. Ann Elizabeth Williamson, née Liddell (1802-78) married Sir Hedworth Williamson (1797-1861), Seventh Bart., in 1826 and lived at Whitburn Hall, Co. Durham. Sir Hedworth Williamson became virtually bankrupt as a result of his ill judged scheme to build docks on the north bank of the Wear in the 1830's. He commissioned Brunel to design and construct the docks, the final cost being £120,000. Dodgson met Frederica and Gertrude Liddell whilst they were staying with their aunt, Lady Williamson, at Whitburn Hall (see *Diary 1*, p. 123 n.*153*).

Cameron Men, etc.[194]

They have got me a bed at Mr. Cust's lodgings: he being away just now.[195]

Sep: 27. (Sat). Nothing happened worth recording during my stay at Whitburn. I left it on Monday the 22nd and left Croft for Whitby at 1.15 this morning, arriving here about 6.30. It has been raining heavily most of the day and a gale is blowing on shore.

Sep: 28.(Sun). In the morning to St. Mary's; I do not know the name of the clergyman who did duty. I met the Bishop's party in returning

---

194.   Dodgson's handwriting for this entry is more difficult to read, not helped by another hand's crossings-out. The songs are not identified.

195.   Daniel Mitford Cust (1821-89), originally with the surname Peacock, was the youngest son of Rev. Daniel Mitford Peacock (1768-1840), rector of Gt. Stainton, Co. Durham; educated at Sedbergh and Christ's, Camb.; B.A. 1845; M.A. 1848; ordained priest 1847; headmaster and chaplain Cirencester Royal Agricultural College 1850; curate Whitburn 1855-7; perpetual curate Netherwitton, Northumberland 1857-63; vicar Seaham Harbour 1863-74; vicar Kirkby Moorside, Yorks. 1874-7; vicar Ripley Derby. 1877-87. He married Sophia Jane Yarker in 1870. This is the same Mr. Cust that Dodgson met on 20 August 1855, and not Rev. Edwards Cust as stated in *Diary 1*, p.120 n.*146*. Rev. Edwards Cust was an older brother who was rector at Danby Wiske. Daniel Mitford Cust was curate at Whitburn in 1855, and therefore fits Dodgson's description. He baptised Dodgson's cousin Clara Menella Wilcox at Whitburn on 26 December 1855. The change in the family name results from the will of Thomas Cust of Danby Hill who died on 14 March 1801. He devised his estates to his nephew, William Peacock, and directed that every person coming into possession of them should assume the surname Cust.

1856

from church: I went again in the afternoon, and heard Mr. Keane[196] preach a very beautiful sermon on "But yet show I unto you a more excellent way."

Sep: 29. (M). Called at the Bainbridges' in the morning, and arranged to have my photographic apparatus taken over there: the children are grown, but otherwise not much altered: the two youngest have their hair dressed in the French fashion, which has an absurd effect. I then called at No. 7, East Terrace, on the Bishop, but he is away for a day or two: however I met the rest of the party on the pier, and they consent very readily to be photographed when I can arrange for them to come over to Hilda Terrace.[197]

---

196.   William Keane (1818-73), seventh son of Robert Keane of County Clare and his wife Jane née Delahunty; educated Charterhouse and Emmanuel, Cambs.; B.A. 1840; M.A. 1843; ordained priest Ely 1843; curate Fenstanton, Cambs. 1843-6; canon St. Paul's Cathedral, Calcutta 1846; Assistant Secretary Missionary Society 1852; perpetual curate Whitby St. Mary 1853-61; rector there from 1862 until his death. He was a Fellow of the Royal Astronomical Society and author of *Hinduism and Romanism*, *The Irish Mission to the Heathen English*, *Public Instruction of Indian Government* and a collection of sermons. He married Elizabeth Fryer Thomas in 1853 and lived at Bagdale, West Terrace, Whitby. They had at least five children.

197.   The Bishop of Ripon, Charles Longley, and his family. See n. *7* and n. *10* above.

While on the pier I stayed to watch an artist who is painting a view of the harbour, and we fell into conversation which ended in his inviting me to come and see his pictures: his name is Witherby.[198]

I dined with the Bainbridges, and met Mrs Pickard and her little girl Adelaide: it being Florence's birthday, I put *Away with Melancholy* in my pocket, and volunteered it as a part of the evening's entertainment.[199] Heavy rain all the evening. Mrs. Pickard gave me a seat in her fly home.

---

198.   Henry Forbes Witherby (1836-1907), artist of landscapes and flowers, exhibited from 1854 at Dudley, Liverpool, Manchester and the Royal Society of British Artists, London. In 1856, he exhibited at the Royal Academy Exhibition and Dodgson might have found his name in the catalogue which he borrowed from Rowley on 22 May. Item 1126 by Witherby is described as "Airey Force, near Ulleswater, Cumberland." Witherby is listed as residing in Highbury Park, Islington. He came from a well-to-do family connected with a long established printing and stationery business in London. He was married to Emily, and they had three sons. His known paintings include; "Study of Spring Flowers" (1854), "The Harvest Moon, Looking Towards Whitby" (1895) and "Fresh from the Kitchen Garden" (1900).

199.   Florence Hilda Bainbridge, born on 29 September 1848, was aged 8 years. No relationship between Mrs. Pickard and the Bainbridges has been established, even though Dodgson hints that Mrs Mary Agnes Bainbridge née Harvey was her sister (see 11 January, above). Mary had two sisters; Sophia Amelia Alexandrina Harvey who married James Archibald Campbell in 1831, and Anne Adelaide Hippolyta Harvey who married George Hobson Bainbridge (possibly Henry's brother) in 1839.

Sep: 30. (Tu). Rain all day. Went with Mr. Bainbridge to see Mr. Witherby's pictures, many of which I admired exceedingly. He paints both in water and oils, and has exhibited for the last three years in the London Exhibitions.

Oct: 1. (W). Spent most of the day photographing.

Oct: 2. (Th). Arranged for the Longleys to come and be photographed and to see Mr. Witherby's pictures. Only Caroline and Rosamond came for the first, and we were joined by the rest of the party on the way to Mr. Witherby's.
Dined in Hilda Terrace.

Oct: 3. (F). Went over with the four Miss Longleys to Hilda Terrace and finished their pictures in spite of the rain. The sky cleared about five, and we went out in a boat, i.e. the Longley party, Miss Lee and myself. Met Trebeck, of Ch. Ch.[200]

Oct: 4. (Sat). Went over again to Hilda Terrace, and took a few pictures, and succeeded in

---

200. James John Trebeck (1837-1904) matriculated at Christ Church in 1855. He gained his B.A. in 1860 and his M.A. in 1883. He was vicar of Annesley, Nottinghamshire, from 1869-71, curate in charge of Southwell Collegiate Church from 1871-81, and rector of Southwell Cathedral Church in 1881.

getting all packed and off by the 12.40 train. Reached Croft 8.30.

Oct: 7. (Tu). Sent off "The Three Voices" to Yates for the *Train*: I sent with it three sketches as suggestions for illustrations.[201]
[Inserted in No. 11, November 1856, but without any illustration.]
I proposed writing "My Uncle" as a continuation of "Novelty and Romancement," and following that up with "My Uncle's Papers," among which the long-intended essay on "Nursery Songs" might be placed.[202]

Oct: 8. (W). Left Croft for Alvaston, which I reached about four o'clock in the afternoon: I found a number of Pooles there, including Mr. Henry Poole and two of his children, Lucy and Ellen, 10 and 8 years old:[203] they were born in Nova Scotia, and have

---

201. The illustrations, as Dodgson notes, did not appear, and have not survived. However, two of them could have been copied into, or from, *Mischmasch*. The manuscript copy is accompanied by two of Dodgson's drawings showing a breeze "lightly bore away his hat" (verse 2) and "proudly folded arm in arm" (verse 17).

202. "My Uncle" and "My Uncle's Papers" did not materialise, although Dodgson began writing preliminary sketches on 21 October.

203. This branch of the Poole family has not been fully identified. The family probably link with Charles Poole (1758-1838) of Stanmore, who married Henrietta Octavia Lutwidge, Dodgson's great aunt.

1856

very un-English looking faces. Aunt Skeffington Poole, from Weston-super-mare, is also staying there.

Oct: 9. (Th). Spent the day in photography, took many pictures of the party, and some of 2 children of Mr. Sherwit the clerk, Mary and Willie.[204]

Oct: 10. (F). Skeffington Hume and Wilfred Longley arrived in time for breakfast, and we left for Oxford in the afternoon: the threefold luggage, all marked with one name, put down at Tom-Gate, caused the wildest scene of confusion I ever witnessed here, and after all we found that no rooms had been allotted to my brothers, who accordingly had to spend the night at the Mitre.[205]

Michaelmas Term 1856

Oct: 11. (Sat). Two or three men called about lectures.

---

204. The clerk at Alvaston, Mr. Sherwit, has not been identified. Dodgson may possibly have recorded an incorrect name.

205. Skeffington and Wilfred matriculated in May, and now entered Christ Church, following in the footsteps of their father and older brother. Accommodation at Christ Church was at a premium during this time, resulting in the two brothers residing at The Mitre, an inn on The High, until rooms could be found for them. Eventually they were allocated rooms in Peckwater Quad, on staircase four, as used by Charles L. Dodgson during his undergraduate days.

Yates wrote the other day to ask leave to abridge "The Three Voices," which I granted: he says it is too long for publication.

[He published it however in full.]

Went in to see the chapel, which is enlarged and much improved: the Dean is staying down at Torquay for his health, and is not expected up for some time.[206]

Oct: 19. (Sun). Dined at Magdalen College with Mr. Barmby.[207] He strongly advises me to read *Never too late to mend*, a novel by one of their Fellows, Charles Reade.[208]

Oct: 21. (Tu). Began writing parts of an article for the *Train*, "My Uncle."

---

206.   The Dean's health was poor during the early years at Christ Church, probably resulting from the unhealthy atmosphere which pervaded the area surrounding Westminster School during his headship there.

207.   James Barmby (1823-?) matriculated at University College in 1841, gained his B.A. in 1845. He became a fellow of Magdalen and took his B.D. there in 1855. He was Mathematical Moderator for the University in 1853. In 1875, he became vicar of Pittington.

208.   *It is Never Too Late to Mend: A Matter of Fact Romance* by Charles Reade (1814-84) was published in 1856. This novel advocated prison reform and created a considerable stir at the time. Reade's most famous novel, *The Cloister and the Hearth: A Tale of the Middle Ages*, did not appear until 1861, but he was already well known for his first book, *Peg Woffington*, published in 1853. He was made Vice-President of Magdalen in 1843, but spent most of his time in London; his interests were theatrical rather than academic.

Oct: 22. (W).   Fell in with Harry and Ina Liddell down in the meadow, and took them up to see my book of photographs: they tell me the Dean is expected back in a week.

Uncle and Aunt T. Raikes called on their way to London with Lizzie (now Mrs. Lowthorpe), and Mr. Lowthorpe, and Lady L. his aunt.[209]

Took Tyrwhitt's photograph unsuccessfully in the afternoon.

Oct: 29. (W).   Went to the Star in the evening to see Miss P. Horton (now Mrs. German Reed) and her husband perform.[210] I thought the whole thing very good: Miss Horton's acting was wonderful, and not the least charm in her performance was her exquisite singing: this especially struck me in Sir John Quill's song *The Fairest of the Fair*, which she sings in a rich tenor, introducing high chest-notes, far sweeter than any man's voice could manage: the

---

209.   Thomas Raikes (1790-1866) married Elizabeth Frances (b. 1800) née Lutwidge (his second wife). She was sister to Dodgson's mother. The Raikes had three children, the youngest was Elizabeth "Lizzie" Lucy Raikes who married Frederick Lowthorpe.

210.   Priscilla Horton (1818-95), actress and singer, in 1844 married Thomas German Reed (1817-88), a musician. In 1855 they began their "Entertainments" in order to provide dramatic amusement for persons reluctant to visit theatres.

whole thing lasted two hours.[211]

Oct: 30. (Th). Went again to the Star, principally to hear *The Fairest of the Fair* sung again, and liked it even better on a second hearing: Skeffington Hume and Wilfred Longley went also.

Missed Heurtley's second lecture by accidentally prolonging my own lectures till half past one: the chances are now decidedly against my completing the course.[212]

Nov: 1. (Sat). Gaudy. Bayne read the Fell speech. The new Fells this year are "Bellett, Mitford, Carey, Girdlestone, and Woodgate." [213]

---

211. Sir John Quil (and not as Dodgson spelt the name) was an invented character in Miss Horton's Entertainment, and his song, *The Fairest of the Fair*, was written by William Brough with music composed by German Reed and based on a Scottish ballad of 1770.

212. Charles Abel Heurtley (1806-95), Lady Margaret Professor of Divinity from 1853 until his death. Dodgson attended Heurtley's lectures on the Creed in May 1855 (see *Diary 1*, p. 91 n. *95*). It was clearly Dodgson's intention to attend Heurtley's lectures on divinity for this term, possibly in preparation for his future ordination.

213. Thomas Vere Bayne read the speech at the Gaudy in honour of Rev. John Fell, one of the early Deans of Christ Church. The Fell Scholars nominated for 1856 were George Bellet, Algernon Mitford, Tupper Carey, Robert Girdlestone and Hamilton Woodgate. For details of Bellet, see *Diary 1*, p. 88 n. *91*. Algernon Bertram Mitford C.B. matriculated at Christ Church in 1855 aged 18. He entered the Foreign Office in 1858 and became Embassy Secretary at St. Petersburgh from 1863-5, Peking 1865-6, Japan 1866 and Secretary to Commissioners of Public Works in 1874. He was J.P. for Batsford Park, Gloucester. Tupper Carey from St.

The Dean dined in Hall, having returned to Oxford a few days ago, thought still far from well. We adjourned afterwards to the Deanery for dessert, and health-drinking. I arranged with the Dean to go over some fine day soon, and have one more try at the view of the cathedral and the children's portraits.

Had young Harington and Shuldham to breakfast as well as Skeffington Hume and Wilfred Longley.[214] I heard from Menella Smedley the other day about Shuldham, who is some kind of relation, being connected through the Humes. He tells me that he is nearly related to Mrs. Norris, wife of the President of Corpus.

Peter's Isle, Guernsey, matriculated at Christ Church in 1842 aged 18, and gained his B.A. in 1846. He was vicar of Ebbesborne Wake, Wiltshire, from 1861 and rural dean in 1863. Robert Baker Girdlestone (1836-1923) became Principal of Wycliffe Hall, Oxford. He was author of many theological works. For a letter dated 7 November 1886 from Dodgson to Girdlestone, see *Letters* p. 646. Hamilton Woodgate from London matriculated in 1854 aged 19.

214.   Richard Harington (1835-1911), second son of Rev. Richard Harington D.D. (1800-53), Principal of Brasenose College, Oxford, and his wife, Cecilia née Smith (see *Diary 1*, p. 88 n. *91*). Edward Barton Shuldham matriculated at Christ Church on 3 May 1856, aged 18, and gained his B.A. in 1862. The family link between Shuldham and Smedley (and hence Dodgson) has not been identified. However, Richard Harington's first daughter, Margaret-Agnata (born 1871), married George Hume Pollock (1870-1924), the first son of Hon. Sir Charles Edward Pollock (1823-97) and his wife, Amy Menella née Dodgson (Dodgson's cousin, daughter of Uncle Hassard).

Nov: 2. (Sun). Took Anderson, of Exeter, into chapel in the afternoon.[215]

Nov: 3. (M). Met Miss Prickett,[216] the governess at the Deanery, walking with Ina, and settled that I would come over on Wednesday morning, if it is fine. I also asked her to try and secure some of the Aclands coming over to be taken: there are five or six of them, and Southey says they are a beautiful family: I have only seen the eldest, Willie.[217]

---

215.   Archibald Anderson from Edinburgh matriculated at Exeter College in 1855 aged 19 and gained his B.A. in 1859 and took his M.A. in 1865.

216.   Mary Prickett (1833-1916), the daughter of James Prickett, the Butler at Trinity College, was employed by the Liddells to be the Governess to their daughters, Lorina, Alice and Edith. The children knew her affectionately as "Pricks."

217.   The Aclands were friends of the Liddells; Sir Henry Wentworth Acland (1815-1900) was Regius Professor of Medicine and honorary physician to the Prince of Wales, and to Prince Leopold when he was at Oxford during 1862. Acland matriculated at Christ Church in 1834 and gained his B.A. in 1840. He was a fellow of All Soul's from 1840-7. He took his B. Med. in 1846 and his D. Med. in 1848. In 1845 he was Lee's reader in anatomy. He married Sarah née Cotton in 1846. He was the Radcliffe librarian in 1851 and natural science examiner in 1857. He was also Dean Liddell's doctor, and gave him advice about his health problems, and even accompanied him on a trip to Madeira for the sake of the Dean's health in 1857 and to Switzerland in 1865. He was knighted in 1884. William Alison Dyke, then aged 9 years, was the first of seven sons. The only daughter was Sarah Angelina, then aged 7 years. The other sons at this time were Henry Dyke aged 6, Theodore Dyke aged 5 and Herbert Dyke aged one year. Reginald Brodie Dyke was born during 1856. Two other sons, Francis Edward Dyke (born 1857) and Alfred Dyke (born 1858) followed.

1856

Began a poem on "Nothing": it may turn out a good subject, but I have not made much of it yet.[218]

Nov: 5. (W). The morning was fair, and I took my camera over to the Deanery, just in time to see the whole party (except Edith) set off with the carriage and ponies, a disappointment for me, as it is the last vacant morning I shall have in the term. However I must manage to clear another morning. I met Dr. Acland today, and he gladly agreed to send over his children to the Deanery to be taken any day I like to appoint.

I have come to the conclusion that it is extravagant to attempt photographs, excepting when success is tolerably certain. I have wasted many pounds this summer, by trying on bad days etc.

Nov: 9. (Sun). Left a note to ask Barmby to dinner any Monday, Wednesday or Friday,

Nov: 10. (M). Clear sun, went to the Deanery to take portraits at two, but the light failed, and I only got one of Harry. I spent an hour or so afterwards with the children and

---

218.   Nothing of Dodgson's poem titled "Nothing" has survived.

governess, up in the schoolroom, making them paper boats etc.

Began a poem which I think of calling "The Sailor's Wife," it will include some stanzas written long ago.[219]

[See Feb: 23, 1857]

Nov: 12. (W). I am becoming embarrassed by the duties of the Lectureship, and must take a quiet review of my position, to see what can be done.

The difficulties are:

I have five pupils, whose lectures need preparing for, namely

Blackmore in for a First at Easter, doing end of Differential Calculus (*new to me*), and to begin Integral Calculus soon.

Rattle in for a First in Mods this time, needs special problems etc. and very probably high Diff: Cal:, a little Int: Cal: and Spherical Trig.

Blore in for a Second, easier problems etc.

Bradshaw in this time [next] year, reading the circle in *Salmon*, and is already in work new to me.

Harrison in for the Junior Scholarship

---

219.   "The Sailor's Wife" appeared in the third volume of *The Train*, pp. 231-3, with an illustration by Charles H. Bennett. In the dramatic poem, a young mother fears for the life of her seafaring husband.

this term, we are beginning *Salmon*, so that his case is included in Bradshaw's, and he is reading with Price as well, which makes his case easier.

Besides these, I want time for some Divinity reading, which is at present entirely dropped, (of course I never get a moment for any other reading, poetry etc.)

Now lectures at present occupy seven hours a day, (always two or three in the evening), so that it is impossible to find time or brain for new reading.

Thus I am daily becoming more and more unfit for the lectureship.[220]

(All this might have remedied in the Long Vacation, but there is no use in regretting that *now*; next Long *must* be devoted to work).

Something must be done, and

---

220.   The role of mathematical lecturer resulted in Dodgson tackling topics he had not thoroughly covered during his reading for the B.A. although he himself had achieved a First. Teaching the more difficult aspects of differential calculus and the complex properties of circles meant that he had to read up on these subjects so that he could be at least one step ahead of his pupils. This is a well known phenomenon when beginning a career in teaching which resolves with experience. A lack of available time added to the pressure which Dodgson felt he was under, exacerbated by his interests in many other subjects. For details of his mathematical students, see *Diary 1*, p. 88 n. *91*. The additional undergraduates included for tuition this term were Robert William Bradshaw (see n. *72* above) and Charles Abbott Brown (see below) who was a servitor in the Cathedral in 1855 who matriculated in January 1856 aged 18, gaining his B.A. in 1860.

done *at once*, or I shall break down altogether.

I have looked over the lectures, to see if they can be abridged; *Parham* and *Brown* both seem likely to give up Mathematics: I am going to speak to their tutors. This would give two spare hours on Monday, Wednesday and Friday morning, and by shifting lectures, I might then clear three evenings a week, which would be an immense gain.

If this fails, these evenings must be cleared some other way.

And I must *at once* set to work and read

(1) *Salmon* right through, doing all the problems.

(2) *Diff: Cal:* all the omitted parts.

(3) *Int: Cal:* commencement.

(4) *Spherical Trig:* right through.

(5) Analyse Mods papers.

(6) Ditto Junior Scholarship.

It would be advisable to consult Price as to what a man ought to have gone through for Moderations and for the Junior Scholarship.[221]

---

221.   Dodgson needed to prepare undergraduates for moderations (preliminary examinations for the B.A.) and the Junior Mathematical Scholarship. His analysis of past papers for moderations provided some guidance. Consulting Professor Bartholomew Price provided Dodgson with further help in preparing undergraduates, particularly for the Junior Scholarship

I must also set apart 6 hours a week to prepare for *Blackmore* and *Bradshaw.*

I strongly think of reading with Price next Long Vacation.

Nov: 14. (F).   Was at the Deanery in the morning taking pictures, and went again in the afternoon by Harry's request to take him and Ina. However I found Mrs. Liddell had said they were not to be taken till all can be taken in a group. This may be meant as a hint that I have intruded on the premises long enough: I am quite of the same opinion myself, and, partly for this reason, partly because I cannot afford to waste any more time on portraits at such a bad season of the year, I have resolved not to go again for the present, nor at all without invitation, except just to pack up the things and bring them back.[222]

---

which he probably never undertook himself, although he did attempt the Senior Mathematical Scholarship (see *Diary 1*, pp. 77-8).

222.   Dodgson took his photographic equipment to the Deanery on 5 November, and spent a number of days attempting photographs, even though, paradoxically, he records the pressures of time caused by his lecturing commitments. The poor light in late autumn resulted in many photographic failures. With little to show for his efforts, Mrs. Liddell may have decided that the intrusion was now unwarranted. He sensed that he had over-stayed his welcome, and chose to withdraw. Within a week he was dining at the Deanery, so the incident was only a transitory dip in the relationship between Dodgson and the Liddells.

> Barmby was to have dined with me, but did not appear. He afterwards sent to say that he was prevented by a friend being with him, and forgot to send me word.

Nov: 15.(Sat). I think of devoting my hour in the Library on Mondays, Wednesdays and Fridays, to reading *Pearson* for Heurtley's lectures.[223] I shall thus have the advantage of having all the original authorities round me to refer to.

Heurtley however has altered the lecture from one to 11, so that I shall be able to take the Library on alternate weeks, as usual.

Nov: 16.(Sun).In the evening to St. Paul's to hear the Revd. John Barclay preach for the Diocesan Education Society.[224] His preaching is eloquent and impressive, though rather more like a speech than a sermon: it was delivered without book, but evidently learnt by heart.

---

223. Charles Abel Heurtley; see n. *185* above. Dodgson owned a copy of Bishop Pearson's *An Exposition of the Creed* revised by Rev. E. Burton in two volumes (Oxford: 1847); see *Library* p. 38 lot 778 & p. 68 lot 207.

224. John Barclay (1817-86) matriculated at Christ Church in 1835 and gained his B.A. in 1840. He was chaplain from 1840-5 and a select preacher in 1856. He became honorary canon of Chester in 1865. He was vicar of Runcorn from 1845 until his death.

Hackman tells me that he (Barclay) was Ruskin's coach, and used to complain of his pupil, that he never could get him to do anything at lecture but talk about water-colour painting.[225]

Nov: 17. (M). Met Willie Acland, and sent my book of photographs by him to Mrs. Acland.

Nov: 19. (W). Dined at the Deanery in the evening, and met (among others) Llewellyn, whose father's book of photographs was shown during the evening. I also met the Dean's father, Mr. Liddell of Easington: he wishes me to take his picture, and I have agreed to go over some fine morning.[226]

Nov: 21. (F). Barmby dined with me.

Elizabeth wrote to me the other

225. Alfred Hackman (1811-74) matriculated at Christ Church in 1832 and gained his B.A. in 1837. He was chaplain from 1837-73, precentor in 1841 and later sub-librarian at the Bodleian in 1862. He was the author of *The Catalogue of the Tanner Manuscripts*. From 1844 until three years before his death he was vicar of St. Paul's, Oxford.

226. John Talbot Dillwyn Llewellyn (1836-?) an undergraduate of Christ Church who matriculated in 1854 from Eton and took a third in physics in 1858. He was a student at the Inner Temple, London, in 1859. He became high sheriff of Penllergare and Ynisygerwn, Glamorgan, in 1887. His father was John Dillwyn Llewellyn, a founder-member of the Photographic Society. His pictures appear in several books illustrated with photographs. The Dean's father was Rev. Henry George Liddell (1788-1872), Rector of Easington. The photograph he requested does not appear to have been taken.

day, asking for suggestions for a Christmas treat for the school, and mentioning a magic lantern. If I could get proper slides for it, a very good plot might be made up out of incidents in a school boy's life, on the model of *The Enraged Musician* (acted by Mr. German Reed).[227]

Nov: 26. (W). I am weary of lecturing and discouraged. I examined six or eight men today who are going in for Little-Go, and hardly one is really fit to go in. It is thankless uphill work, goading unwilling men to learning they have no taste for, to the inevitable neglect of others who really want to get on.

[*Memorandum* - to lay out work for this Christmas Vacation.]

Nov: 28. (F). Went to a musical party at the Deanery in the evening to meet the new Bishop of Durham.[228]

---

227. The magic lantern was subsequently purchased by Dodgson, see 13 December, and a slide show was undertaken to entertain the children at Croft School as requested by his sister, Elizabeth, at the end of the year. Dodgson used voices and characters from various plays and entertainments he had previously experienced in a plot of his own devising.

228. Dodgson already knew the new Bishop of Durham well, for he was his father's great friend, Charles Longley, currently Bishop of Ripon. See n. 7 above.

1856

Dec: 1. (M).   Dined with Fowler in Common Room at Lincoln to meet Charsley of Ch. Ch. who is living at Iffley.[229]

Dec: 2. (Tu).   Sudden death of Dr. Hussey:[230] It is said to have been caused by disease of the heart. I was to have gone to Dr. Bull's this evening, but the party is put off.[231]

Dec: 3. (W).   Went to bring some things from the Deanery, and called on Mrs. Liddell, taking with me the two portraits which I left with Mrs. Bullar in the summer to be coloured, (and which she had done by a professional artist). She talks of sending Harry to Twyford at Easter, and took me into the school-room to see specimens of his sums and Latin: in the former he is well on.[232]

---

229.   William Henry Charsley (1820-1900) matriculated at Christ Church in 1837. He gained his B.A. in 1850 at St. Mary Hall and took his M.A. at Christ Church in 1851. He was a licensed master of Charsley Hall.

230.   Dr. Robert Hussey (1803-56), Student of Christ Church, first Regius Professor of Ecclesiastical History.

231.   Dr. John Bull (1790-1858), Canon of Christ Church, and formerly Censor and Treasurer. He gained his B.A. in 1812, M.A. in 1814, B.D. in 1821 and D.D. in 1825. He was elected proctor in 1820.

232.   Harry eventually went to Twyford School, and Dodgson met him there during a visit in December 1857.

1856

Met Mrs. Acland and Lady .....
there.[233]

I spent the evening at Mrs. Litton's with Wilfred and Synnot. I especially admired a song she sang, new to me, *Oh swallow, swallow* from Tennyson.[234]

I saw at Bayne's the other day what appeared to be very good arrangements of operas for one performer. They are by Devaux, and sold by Cramer and Beale.[235]

Dec: 4. (Th). Got a long table for my larger sitting-room.

Dec: 8. (M). Collections began.[236]

Dec: 12. (F). Collections over: went up to London with Skeffington and Wilfred, and put up at the Northumberland Hotel.

---

233. The Lady is not identified.

234. Mrs Litton and Synnot are not identified. "O Swallow, Swallow, flying, flying South" is from Tennyson's poem, *The Princess. A Medley*, first published in 1847.

235. The operas for one performer by Devaux have not been identified.

236. Collections; end of term examinations at Oxford University.

1856

Called at the Deanery before starting. The Dean and Mrs. L. are going abroad for four months, for his health. The children are to remain in Oxford: Lloyd has undertaken to teach Harry his Latin and Greek. I offered to teach him sums etc. but Mrs. L. seemed to think it would take up too much of my time.

Christmas Vacation

Dec: 12. (F). Arrived at the Northumberland hotel about six: we went there by Liddon's advice, but it is a wretched little place, more like a public house.

Went to Exeter Hall to hear the *Messiah*. Mrs. Clare Hepworth, who had the treble part, was too unwell to go through it, and a Miss Louisa Vinnings finished it. The change was decidedly for the better, as her voice is delicious: it was stated to be the first time she had sung a solo in public.[237]

Dec: 13. (Sat). Uncle Hassard called, and by his advice we changed our quarters in the course of the day to the Golden Cross.

---

237.   Dodgson's second visit during the year at Exeter Hall to hear Handel's *Messiah*, see 18 March above.

1856

Chose a Magic Lantern and slides at Watkin and Hill's for the Croft school.

In the afternoon we went to Miss P. Horton at the Gallery of Illustration, and in the evening to the Adelphi - *Janet Pride*, a regular Adelphi drama, and a very pretty extravaganza, *The Statue Bride, or the Elves.*[238]

Dec: 14.(Sun). Spent the day at Putney.

Dec: 15. (M). Bought a quantity of toys for the schools at the German bazaar, Portland Place. Dined with Uncle Skeffington in Brompton who showed us a curious new French toy, the "Orthoscope." In the evening to the Olympic - *Wives as they were, and maids as they are*, a stupid old comedy of Mrs. Inchbald's, but extremely well acted, and *Jones the Avenger*, in which Robson's acting was a perfect treat.[239]

Dec: 16. (Tu). Visited Albert Smith in the afternoon, and the Princess' in the evening - *Midsummer*

---

238. *Janet Pride* was a four-act drama by Dion Boucicault (1822-90). *The Statue Bride, or The Elves* was an anonymous "fairy spectacle," but possibly by Vincent Amcott who wrote the words for an opera of this name which was produced ten years later, with music by Aspa.

239. *Wives as they were, and Maids as they are* was a comedy by Elizabeth Inchbald (1753-1821). *Jones the Avenger* was an anonymous farce.

Night's Dream, the scenes in which were beautiful almost beyond description, but there is very little acting, or opportunity for acting, in the play. Harley was amusing as "Bottom," and Miss C. Leclerque made a beautiful "Titania": "Puck" was very cleverly acted by the little Ellen Terry, who was "Mamillius" in *The Winter's Tale* exactly six months ago. The second piece was *Our Wife, or the Rose of Amiens* in which Miss C. Leclerque, Harley, and Fisher appeared.[240]

Dec: 17. (W). Returned to Oxford, my chief reason being that Rattle is going in for Honours in Moderations on Saturday, and I wish to give him as much help as possible.[241]

---

240. Albert Smith (1816-60), author of *Christopher Tadpole* (1848), was well known for his theatrical entertainments. John Pritt Harley (1786-1858), an opera singer who became an actor and excelled in the roles of Shakespearean clowns. Carlotta Leclerque (1840?-93) made a name for her Shakespearean heroines, Titania being her first, and later toured America with Charles Fechter. *Our Wife, or, The Rose of Amiens* was a comedy drama in two acts by John Maddison Morton. David Fisher (1816?-87), second of three actors of that name, being the son of the first and the father of the third. His chief roles included Mr. Micawber, and Brigard in *Frou-Frou*; his last appearance was in *Twelfth Night* at the Lyceum in 1884, as Sir Toby Belch, with both Henry Irving and Ellen Terry in the cast.

241. With Dodgson's support, Henry Rattle gained a second class in mathematical moderations.

Called at the Heurtleys in the morning, (having dined there on the 10th), and left my book of photographs with Mrs. Heurtley.

Dec: 18. (Th). Called at the Deanery, and took Harry a Christmas box, a mechanical tortoise: (I gave Ina one the other day, *Mrs. Rutherford's Children*).[242] The Dean and Mrs. L. intend leaving on Saturday: they are going to Madeira.

Went to Badcock's with Scoltock, and chose a wall-paper for my larger room: I am having the ceiling white-washed etc. at the same time.

Dec: 19. (F). Began the Common Room File-book, which turns out a much longer job than I expected.[243]

Dec: 20. (Sat). Breakfast with Prout. Sent for wall paper patterns to
Crase and Co.

---

242. *Mrs Rutherford's Children* by Elizabeth Wetherell, pseudonym of Susan Bogert Warner (1819-85).

243. The purpose of the Common Room File-book is unknown but probably constituted a book containing minutes of meetings. Apparently, it has not survived. Dodgson became Curator of the Common Room in 1882, an honorary but onerous position at Christ Church, which he held for just over nine years. During this time he kept a notebook of all decisions made at meetings of the Common Room, and this has survived.

1856

Wigmore Street,
Cavendish Square
by Sandford's advice. Sent also to Watkin
and Hill, Charing Cross, to arrange to buy
the Magic Lantern.

Dec: 21.(Sun). Breakfast with Marshall. Took Andrews
to Common Room.

Dec: 22. (M). Breakfast with Tyrwhitt.
The Dean and Mrs. Liddell started
for Madeira, with Dr. Acland, who is
going to accompany them there.

Dec: 23. (Tu). Met Harry and Ina in the Quadrangle,
coming home from riding, and went into
the Deanery with them, and stayed
luncheon, (or rather their dinner). Dined
with Dr. Bull, and met, besides the
Masters who are up, the Auditor, Gerwain
Lavie.[244] Went to Tyrwhitt's afterwards:
he showed me some of his poetry, both
original and translation: both I like very
much.

---

244. Gerwain Lavie (1836-?) was a Westminster student at Christ Church
between 1854-61. He took his B.A. in 1858 gaining a fourth in classics
and a fourth in law and history. He became a solicitor in 1861 and a
registrar in Chancery in 1882. Apparently, he was invited, as an
undergraduate with integrity who had just gained a first in classics
moderations, to audit the Christ Church finances.

Dec: 24. (W). Was up till half past five packing, and as it was not then worth while going to bed, I spent the remainder of the night, till half past six, in an arm-chair. Left Oxford by the 8.15 train and arrived at Croft about 8 p.m.

Dec: 26. (F). The day fixed for the magic lantern: it turned out stormy, and the lantern did not arrive. We decided on having two exhibitions, instead of one, on Wednesday and Thursday.

Dec: 30. (Tu). School feast - began about half past one with singing of various kinds. The feast itself did not take long. It was followed by the cutting up of a "bran-pie," containing sweetmeats for all the children, and toys for the younger ones. In spite of the bad weather nearly 150 children came: the distribution went off with much less confusion than the Christmas tree of last year.

Dec: 31. (W). First exhibition of the Magic Lantern, the largest audience I ever had, about 80 children, and a large miscellaneous party besides of friends, servants etc.

I expected the whole thing to last about an hour and a half, so as to be over soon after three. As it turned out, it did not begin till two, instead of half past

1856

one, and lasted till nearly half past four. I divided it into two parts, of 24 and 23 pictures, with a rest of about half an hour between. I introduced 13 songs in the course of the performance, six for myself, and seven for the children; and employed seven different voices (Wright, Madame Celeste, Miss Snowberry and the organ boy from Miss P. Horton's entertainment, Mooney and Spooney, and Mr. Trimmer out of *Away with Melancholy*).[245]

As a whole I think it proved successful, though the first part was rather too long: several of the views may safely be omitted in the next performance.

Half past eleven: Now at the close of the Old Year, let me review the past and take counsel with myself for the future. I must with sorrow confess that my bad habits are almost unchanged. I am afraid that lately I have been even more irregular than ever, and more averse to exertion: though the labour of last term has been

---

245.   Dodgson must have enjoyed imitating various voices as part of the Croft School entertainment, inspired, no doubt, by his frequent visits to the theatre and similar entertainments. "Mooney and Spooney" are characters he used in *La Guida di Bragia* (c. 1850). The voice of Mr. Trimmer, clearly one of his favourites, was solemn even when excited. The contradiction probably appealed to his sense of humour.

nearly as heavy as at any period in my life, it has been forced on me by my position, rather than taken up voluntarily.

{The next whole page of the journal is missing. See "Introduction" above, pp. 4-5}

As to the future, I may lay down as absolute necessities, *Divinity Reading*, and *Mathematical Reading*. I trust to do something this Vacation, but most of the Long Vacation must be devoted to work, and I think my best plan will be to take lodgings wherever Price has his reading party and so get occasional help from him. On other subjects I think there is no use in making resolutions, (I hope to make good progress in Photography in the Easter Vacation: it is my one recreation, and I think should be done well).

I do trust most sincerely to amend myself in those respects in which the past year has exhibited the most grievous shortcomings, and I trust and pray that the most merciful God may aid me in this and all other good undertakings. Midnight is past: bless the New Year, oh heavenly Father, for thy dear Son Jesus Christ's sake!

1856

Index

Page numbers are given, but if the reference is within a footnote, this will be indicated immediately following the page number in italics.

Notes

158

Notes